TAKE CONTROL OF YOUR DESTINY

Since the appearance of *Practical Candleburning Rituals* in 1970, thousands of people have brought about positive changes in their lives with the simple but effective techniques of candle magick. Now you can explore the more involved and effective techniques of *Advanced Candle Magick*.

Here are more powerful rituals that go beyond the simple spells offered in *Practical Candleburning Rituals*. Explore a wide array of advanced techniques derived from a variety of sources and discover a wealth of new ways to empower and transform your life through candle magick.

More involved than the rituals offered in *Practical Candleburning Rituals,* here are spells and ceremonies to dramatically improve your confidence, contact spirit guides, start a new job or lose a bad habit, and even to find the perfect mate.

Prepare yourself with ritual baths, consecrated oils, mental and physical exercise—even specific diets to maximize your success. Use astrology, color symbolism, and other magickal techniques to boost the effectiveness of your spells. Learn the secrets of making your own candles and working with herbs and stones to enhance your rituals.

Ray Buckland shows you how to make candle magick an integral and rewarding part of your lifestyle—no matter your religious background or prior experience.

About the Author

RAYMOND BUCKLAND has been interested in the occult and matters metaphysical for fifty years; has been actively involved in various aspects of the subject for forty years; and has been writing about it for nearly thirty years. He has written more than twenty-five books, has lectured and presented workshops across the United States, and has appeared on major television and radio shows nationally and internationally. He has also written screenplays, been a technical advisor for films, and appeared in films and videos.

Ray comes from an English Romany (Gypsy) family and presently resides, with his wife Tara, on a small farm in central Ohio. After writing, his other passion is homebuilt airplanes.

To Write to the Author

If you wish to contact the author or would like more information about this book, please write to the author in care of Llewellyn Worldwide, and we will forward your request. Both the author and publisher appreciate hearing from you and learning of your enjoyment of this book. Llewellyn Worldwide cannot guarantee that every letter written to the author will be answered, but all will be forwarded. Please write to:

Raymond Buckland
℅ Llewellyn Worldwide
2143 Wooddale Drive
Woodbury, MN 55125-2989

Please enclose a self-addressed stamped envelope for reply, or $1.00 to cover costs. If outside U.S.A., enclose international postal reply coupon.

LLEWELLYN'S PRACTICAL MAGICK SERIES

ADVANCED CANDLE MAGICK

MORE SPELLS AND RITUALS FOR EVERY PURPOSE

RAY BUCKLAND

LLEWELLYN PUBLICATIONS
WOODBURY, MINNESOTA

FIRST EDITION
Twenty-sixth Printing, 2022

Cover Photograph: Leo Tushaus
Cover Design: Lynne Menturweck
Illustrations by the Author
Book Design and Layout: Designed To Sell

Library of Congress Cataloging in Publication Data
Buckland, Raymond.
    Advanced candle magick : more spells and rituals
    for every purpose / Raymond Buckland. -- 1st ed.
       p. cm. (Llewellyn's practical magick series)
    Includes bibliographical references.
    ISBN 13: 978-1-56718-103-6
    ISBN 10: 1-56718-103-1 (pbk.)
    1. Magic. 2. Rites and ceremonies. 3. Candles and
    lights.   I. Title.   II. Series.
BF1623.R6B76   1996
   133.4--dc20   95-49693
                                        CIP

Llewellyn Worldwide does not participate in, endorse, or have any authority or responsibility concerning private business transactions between our authors and the public.
    All mail addressed to the author is forwarded but the publisher cannot, unless specifically instructed by the author, give out an address or phone number.

Llewellyn Publications
A Division of Llewellyn Worldwide Ltd.
2143 Wooddale Drive
Woodbury, Minnesota 55125-2989
www.llewellyn.com
Llewellyn is a registered trademark of Llewellyn Worldwide Ltd.
Printed in the United States of America

LLEWELLYN'S PRACTICAL MAGICK SERIES

To some people, the idea that "Magick" is practical comes as a surprise.

It shouldn't. The entire basis for Magick is to exercise influence over one's environment. While Magick is also, and properly so, concerned with spiritual growth and psychological transformation, even the spiritual life must rest firmly on material foundations.

The material world and the psychic are intertwined, and it is this very fact that establishes the Magickal Link: that the psychic can as easily influence the material as vice versa.

Magick can, and should, be used in one's daily life for better living! Each of us has been given Mind and Body, and surely we are under Spiritual obligation to make full usage of these wonderful gifts. Mind and Body work together, and Magick is simply the extension of this interaction into dimensions beyond the limits normally conceived. That's why we commonly talk of the "supernormal" in connection with domain of Magick.

The Body is alive, and all Life is an expression of the Divine. There is God-power in the Body and in the Earth, just as there is in Mind and spirit. With Love and Will, we use Mind to link these aspects of Divinity together to bring about change.

With Magick we increase the flow of Divinity in our lives and in the world around us. We add to the beauty of it all—for to work Magick we must work in harmony with the Laws of Nature and of the Psyche. Magick is the flowering of the Human Potential.

Practical Magick is concerned with the Craft of Living well and in harmony with Nature, and with the Magick of the Earth, in the things of the Earth, in the seasons and cycles and in the things we make with hand and Mind.

OTHER BOOKS BY THE AUTHOR

Witchcraft...the Religion (Buckland Museum, 1966)
A Pocket Guide to the Supernatural (Ace, 1969)
Witchcraft Ancient and Modern (HC, 1970)
Practical Candleburning Rituals (Llewellyn, 1970, 1976, 1982)
Witchcraft from the Inside (Llewellyn, 1971, 1975, 1995)
Here Is the Occult (House of Collectibles, 1974)
The Tree: Complete Book of Saxon Witchcraft (Weiser, 1974)
Anatomy of the Occult (Weiser, 1977)
The Magick of Chant-O-Matics (Parker, 1978)
Practical Color Magick (Llewellyn, 1983)
Buckland's Complete Book of Witchcraft (Llewellyn, 1986)
Secrets of Gypsy Fortunetelling (Llewellyn, 1988)
Buckland's Gypsy Fortunetelling Deck (Llewellyn, 1989)
Gypsy Dream Dictionary (Llewellyn, 1990, 1998)
Secrets of Gypsy Love Magick (Llewellyn, 1990)
Scottish Witchcraft (Llewellyn, 1991)
Buckland's Book of Spirit Communications
   formerly *Doors to Other Worlds* (Llewellyn, 1993, 2004)
Ray Buckland's Magic Cauldron (Galde Press, 1995)
Truth About Spirit Communication (Llewellyn, 1995)
Gypsy Witchcraft & Magic (Llewellyn, 1998)
Coin Divination (Llewellyn, 2000)
Buckland's Romani Tarot (Llewellyn, 2001)
Solitary Séance (Llewellyn, 2010)

FICTION
The Committee (Llewellyn, 1993)
Cardinal's Sin (Llewellyn, 1996)

VIDEO
Witchcraft Yesterday and Today (Llewellyn, 1990)

CONTENTS

FIGURES

For Tara

*Many thanks to Marlene Skilken,
Donald Michael Craig, and
Debbie Stinner for helpful information.*

INTRODUCTION
Low Magick; High Magick

My book, *Practical Candleburning,* was first published
in 1970. Since that time it has gone through three
editions—changing its name slightly to *Practical Candleburning Rituals*—sold well over 200,000 copies (to
date; it's still in print) and been translated into several
foreign languages. This reflects that there is a constant
interest in Magick and in candleburning Magick specifically. Indeed, candleburning has been done for centuries, if not millennia; and the reason it has been done
for so long is that it works! *It is effective.*

One of the attractions of candleburning is the sim-
plicity of its working. It is what might be termed "Low
Magick"—the Magick of the people. (The Magick of
Witchcraft—the old religion of the common people—was
always Low Magick.) It requires no special tools, and no
great investment of money, time, or learning. Since the
candleburning Magick I presented in that earlier book
has served so well, why present another version?

Simply as a choice. In contrast to Low Magick, there
is, as might be expected, High Magick. A good example
of High Magick is what is usually termed Ceremonial,
or Ritual, Magick. This is a form that requires a great
deal of preparation. Elaborate tools are required, which
must be made to very specific formulae. A great deal of
time and expense is necessary, as is a certain level of

intelligence. Some rituals of High Magick have taken years to perform. Indeed, some Ceremonial Magicians have worked a lifetime striving to achieve just one particular Magickal goal.

If Low Magick can achieve the same things as High Magick, why would anyone go to all the time and expense of High Magick when they could do it the easier way? That's a little like asking why someone would pay $200,000 for a Rolls Royce to drive around, when they can pick up a second-hand Volkswagen for less than $2,000! Quality of travel aside, both will get you where you want to go; it's all a matter of personal preference. That's really all it is in Magick.

As with the Rolls Royce-Volkswagen simile, there are technical differences, but both can be effective. Some people will continue to prefer the simple, basic rituals of candleburning I presented in *Practical Candleburning Rituals,* but others are going to prefer what is offered here. The rituals in this book are far more complex than the earlier ones. There is much more preparation before the rituals can even be started. Yet for some people this is all part of Magick; the preparation is an integral part of the rituals. To make special robes to wear for the rites, to construct the working place or Magickal Study in exacting detail, to actually fashion the very candles themselves so that they meet all the requirements—these are all added ingredients that some feel may make the difference between success and failure. The Volkswagen will carry you from A to B, yes, but in the Rolls Royce there is the comfort of knowing that, although there can be no absolute guarantees against breakdown, every possible item has been covered.

Both High Magick and Low Magick can be effective. As I've stated above, which you choose is a matter of personal preference. Choose that which gives you the greatest confidence; that with which you are most comfortable working.

PART ONE

WHAT IS MAGICK?

I

Magick and Responsibility

Magick is not just something from out of the past with no place in the present. It can be as much a part of today as is a television set, a computer, or a turbo-charged sports car. So long as we have things which we desire and events that we wish to happen, there is a place for Magick in our lives. In fact, Magick can bring us that television set, computer, or sports car!

You don't have to be a Witch (or a Jew, Buddhist, Moslem, or whatever) to do Magick. Magick is a practice, not a religion, although many religions do use Magick as part of their beliefs and practices. You do not have to hold any particular religious beliefs to do Magick. Anyone can do Magick; anyone can be a Magician; anyone can do candleburning Magick.

What is Magick?

Making something that you want happen.

Creating your own reality.

Words and actions affecting physical reality.

A seemingly unnatural happening brought about by human means.

"The science or art of causing change to occur in conformity with the Will." *(Aleister Crowley)*

All of the above are acceptable definitions of Magick. Events normally happen following a course of cause-and-effect, although we are invariably unaware of this principle as life flows by in a seemingly haphazard manner. If we can interrupt this flow—this "disorganized pattern"—and *make* an event occur when and where we want it, then that is Magick. We are making something happen that we want to happen.

Magick can be done by individuals or by groups and there are probably dozens of different forms: "High" Magick; "Low" Magick; imitative or sympathetic; ceremonial or ritual; various religious forms; negative and positive (or "black" and "white"). Your choice may depend upon your need—love, health, wealth, power, or protection—but to work Magick is to take on responsibility.

Ethics of Magick

A so-called "Black" Magician (nothing to do with race) is one who has no ethics where Magick is concerned. He or she has no qualms about interfering with another's free will. A young woman in love, who sets out to work a spell to draw a particular young man to her, would be included under this heading; she would be a black, or negative, magician! Her goal is to draw that man to her *whether he will or no*, which is to interfere with his free will. This is perhaps the best criterion upon which to judge Magick as either white (positive) or black (negative). Is your intention to interfere with another's free will? If so, regardless of your reasons, you should not do it. It's as simple as that.

Of course, when it comes right down to it, we are manipulating people in just about everything we do in our daily lives! Just to wish someone a good day is to put the thought in their mind that they will have one (manipulation does not have to be negative). To give advice to someone is to put pressure, however slight, upon them to change. Even this type of manipulation is interfering with the person's free will; so you see how careful you must be in gauging the effect of Magick?

To work healing Magick is very definitely to manipulate. You are deliberately setting out to change the person who needs the healing. Is it right that you do so? Is the suffering perhaps because of some lesson that needs to be learned? Are you then playing God/dess?

One way around this is to always ask permission of the person before doing Magick for him or her—even healing Magick. You might also attempt to put yourself in the other person's place before doing anything which will affect him or her. In the case of healing, you would probably feel good about the effort being made, but in other cases, such as love spells, it's not as obvious.

It would seem that manipulation is sometimes unavoidable, especially in the case of healings. Let me therefore re-emphasize that whatever sort of Magick you are planning to do, spend some time examining the full, far-reaching effects it will have. If it is going to harm anyone in any way, don't do it; find a different way to achieve the same end.

It's not always easy to see what repercussions a Magickal act may have. Who is likely to be touched by the changes which you are trying to bring about? How far-reaching will the influence of your Magick be? Many times there can be a domino effect. Therefore, Magick is a discipline which, to be done correctly, needs to be carefully planned and executed. This is why Magick should never be done lightly, and never in a hurry.

Historical Perspective

It is unfortunate that so many powerful acts of Magick which have occurred throughout history have been of the negative variety. In ancient Egyptian times (c. 1200 B.C.E.), an Egyptian treasury official worked harmful Magick against the Pharaoh Rameses III using a wax image of him. Francis, Earl Bothwell, did the same thing through the agencies of the Berwick coven of Witches, hoping to get rid of King James VI of Scotland and take over the throne. In seventeenth-century France, Catherine de Medici, wife of King Henri II and mother of succeeding kings Francis II, Charles IX, and Henri III, was rumored to have used substantial Magick to bring her sons to the throne and keep them there.

Positive Magick was used by Witches to turn back invasions of England by the Spanish Armada in 1588, and Adolf Hitler's military in more recent times.

A number of individuals were famous (or infamous) in the history of Magick during the last several centuries. Theophrastus Paracelsus, magician-alchemist and giant of the Renaissance, was prominent in early sixteenth-century Europe, as was Henry Cornelius Agrippa, a disciple of Paracelsus. Jacob Böhme, who tried to show how good and evil come from the heart of reality, Robert Fludd, and Joseph Balsamo (known as Count Cagliostro) were all major European Magicians. MacGregor Mathers, Arthur Edward Waite, and the poet W. B. Yeats led Magickal thinking in the late nineteenth century. They were later joined by Aleister Crowley and Israel Regardie.

II

MAGICK HOLDS NO GUARANTEES

Over the years I've received many letters from people who have done candleburning Magick, color Magick, and chanting. Most have had wonderful things to report about how successful they were and how their life was changed; but there have also been those who complained that, no matter how hard they tried, they didn't get the results they wanted.

Unfortunately, *there are no guarantees with Magick.* We can do everything correctly—use the right incense, the correct time of the month, perfectly colored candles—and still get nothing! Why is that?

One point of view is that the gods (God/Goddess/All-That-Is, depending upon your personal beliefs) are watching over us and have certain things planned. For example, a deserted wife may do all in her power to bring about the return of her husband (actually a "no-no"—see Chapter One), but to no avail. The reason is that the gods know he's a no-good deadbeat and she's far better off without him! Not only that, but they have a wonderful, ideal mate for her waiting in the wings, if she will only be patient until the time is right.

Actually, the time that it takes for Magick to work can have a bearing on our belief as to whether or not it worked at all. Sometimes the results are a long time in coming. There are many of us—myself included—who have found just such a scenario, but only recognized it in retrospect. At the time we think "why me?" or "why not me?" or perhaps "why isn't this working?" or "what have I done wrong?" It's only many weeks, months, or even years later that we can look back and say, "Oh! So that's why it didn't work!" (I'll talk more about this in Chapter Three.)

Perhaps the most frustrating situations are those centered on love. A man yearns for a certain woman, or a woman for a particular man. They do candle Magick but nothing happens; there is no "Magickal flash" bringing them together. Let's examine such a situation for a moment.

Jane Smith worships Frank Wilson from afar, but he doesn't seem to know she's alive. The temptation is for her to work Magick to bring him to her, but we know that wouldn't be right since it would interfere with his free will. What should she do? Jane should start by making a list of all the qualities that she likes about

Frank. She should then modify the list to be all the qualities she would like to find in "the perfect mate." She might want a tall, blond, physically well-developed male with an interest in metaphysics, jazz, nature, and sailing, who is also a great dancer and classic-movie buff. If Frank fits this description, fine, but if not, she should not compromise. She should do her Magick to bring to her this "ideal mate"—not Frank specifically. If it turns out that Frank does fit the description, he may well suddenly notice her and take an interest; but it is just as likely that there is someone else (perhaps someone who has been worshipping Jane from afar, and whom *she* didn't know existed!) who fits the description even better, and who then appears on the scene.

By limiting your goal, such as by naming an individual, you are limiting your chances for success. It's something of a contradiction, but you need to be very *general* in what you aim for, and yet very specific. I'll talk more about this later.

III

SYMPATHETIC MAGICK

Candleburning Magick is based on what is known as sympathetic Magick. We find the earliest examples of this 25,000 years ago in the Paleolithic preparations for hunting and fertility. By making a large, clay figure of a bear (or whichever animal was to be hunted), and by then sticking it with spears, early humans believed they would be able to influence the hunt which was to follow. They thought—indeed, they strongly *believed*—that the real hunt would go exactly as did the ritual hunt, and that they would successfully kill their prey. Similarly, they constructed almost life-sized, clay representations of two bison copulating, believing that this would cause the real bison to do the same, and ensure a continued food supply. Examples of these Magickal tools have been found in caves in the south of France and Spain.

In ancient Egypt, in 350 B.C.E., King Nectanebo II fought his battles in advance by making wax figures of his and his enemy's ships, and acting out the conflict to come—ensuring that he won, of course! He, too, believed that the real battle would duplicate his enacted one. From the earliest times there has been a tradition that says, if you have a figure which represents something real, whatever you do to that figure will cause the same thing to happen to who or what it represents. In other words, one is "in sympathy" with the other. This is the origin of sympathetic Magick.

We are all familiar with the black Magick doll stuck with pins, sometimes referred to erroneously as a "Voodoo doll." (This is not peculiar to followers of Voudoun, but is found universally.) The idea behind it is to make an image of a specific person, and then to bring pain or death to that person by sticking the doll with pins or melting it in front of a fire. Candle Magick is sympathetic Magick using candles to represent the participants in what is to be achieved. Candles also symbolize things such as Success, Money, Love, and Protection. By manipulating these candles you show what it is that you desire—for example, to bring success to yourself (moving one candle toward the other), or to draw love to a person (advancing two candles until they meet and join). It is the same principle as the "Voodoo doll," but working in a positive way.

What sort of results you can expect from your rituals is a hard question to answer, since there are no guarantees in Magick, as I pointed out in Chapter Two. Certainly there will be no "flash and a bang" with immediate, on-the-spot results. Usually you can expect to see the effects of your Magick anywhere from three days to a month later.

Some rituals can be done just once, while others need to be repeated over a period of time. The longer-working rituals don't necessarily need more time to show results, however; their effectiveness is in the build-up of power over time which can be far more potent than the results of one-time rituals.

Methods developed by many generations of candle-burners dictate what is to be used to depict what. This is especially true where colors are concerned. In my earlier candle book we worked almost exclusively with color as a means of identification. In this book we will keep the traditional color symbolism, while examining more advanced techniques.*

Magick is a Power

Magick is a nebulous term. We've looked at definitions of the word, but these don't really help us to understand

*See Raymond Buckland, *Practical Color Magick* (Llewellyn Publications, 1983) for details of color and its properties.

exactly what it is. Magick is a "power" of a sort. It is not electrical, although there have been many attempts to measure it as an electrical current, with some claims of success. It is probably closest to electricity in the ways it works, and that certainly serves as an excellent analogy. Electricity is a force which can be used for good or evil. It can bring power to a computer, a television set, lights and heaters, cooking stoves, and even automobiles. It can also be used for electric chairs to execute, for weapons of war, and destruction. So, in itself, electricity is neither good nor evil, and that's exactly how it is with Magick: It is a powerful force which can be used for good or evil depending upon the Magician.

Magick is energy which can be created by anyone. It is not only certain, special people who can work Magick; we all have the ability to produce this power to change things. Certainly some people seem more able than others to do this, but through practice we all can become expert.

A combination of *need* and *will power* is all that is necessary to do Magick. If you ask someone else to work Magick for you—even an accomplished Magician—it is unlikely that he or she will be able to produce the results that you could. The reason is that the Magician does not have the personal connection you have—the need for the Magick to succeed. For example, you are out of work and almost out of money. You need some income to put food on the table and keep the roof over your head. You are desperate! You go to a friend of a friend who has some sort of a reputation as a dabbler in the occult. Surely she can help. She listens to your story and promises to work for you, but no luck. Why?

No matter how much she empathizes, this Magician does not have the driving *need* you have for the Magick to succeed. If it doesn't work, you are the one who is homeless and starving; she can simply shrug her shoulders with regret. So, even though you are not the expert, you are the one to do the Magick. You are the one who will put every last ounce of energy into it because your very life is at stake. You will produce more Magick than she through your need and your will power—the will for it to succeed.

Therefore, Magick should be done by the one whom it will affect—the one we call "the Petitioner."

Part Two

Working Candle Magick

IV

TIMING RITUALS FOR BEST RESULTS

Using every possible advantage to ensure success, the timing of your rituals is critical. By timing, I mean the actual hour of the day, day of the week, position in the month, and time of the year in which the ritual is performed.

The ancients paid special attention to determining favorable times to begin the erection of important edifices. Once commenced, the existence of the building, or anything, tends to correspond to the conditions under which it was begun. The ancients were just as meticulous in their choice of starting times for Magickal operations. Succeeding Magicians, over many centuries, have continued the practice, and what has served them so well for so long is certainly worthy of our consideration.

The Significance of Ritual Times

Hours of the Day

Each hour of the day is ruled by a planet, and the nature of that time of day corresponds to the nature of that planet. Not only can you initiate important matters according to the appropriate planetary hour, but you can judge the nature of a matter (a letter you receive, for example) by the planetary hour in which you first became aware of, or came into contact with it.

The nature of each planetary hour is the same as the description of each of the planets. You will not need to refer to the descriptions for Uranus, Neptune, and Pluto, however, since they are considered here to be higher octaves of Mercury, Venus, and Mars, respectively. (If something is ruled by Uranus, you can use the description of the hour of Mercury, for Neptune use Venus, and for Pluto use Mars.)

The only other factor you need to know to use the planetary hours is the time of your local Sunrise and Sunset on any given day. You can get this from your daily newspaper. Having determined the times of Sunrise and Sunset, you divide the daylight, and then the nighttime, each into twelve *equal parts* (not twelve sixty-minute hours). They will rarely turn out to be sixty-minute hours because, during our summer there is more daylight than night, and during the winter more night than day. Having charted the times when each of these periods occurs, you can now ascribe to each period its planetary rulership. (See Table 1, "Planetary Hours," and Table 2, "Properties of Planets," in the Appendix.)

Days of the Week

The days of the week are associated with particular attributes, generally based on the planets and the ancient deities associated with them. For example, Friday is associated with both the planet and the goddess Venus. Since Venus is the Goddess of Love, Friday is the best day for dealing with anything to do with love. (See Table 3, "Days, Planetary Rulers, and Attributes," in the Appendix.)

Time of the Month

For the time of the month, we look at the phases of the Moon. Anything to do with increase—money, love, business, improving health, or promotion—needs to be done in the waxing cycle of the moon, from new moon to full moon. Anything to do with loss—losing weight, stopping smoking, disassociation, or separation—needs to be done in the waning cycle, from full moon to new moon.

Time of the Year

For rituals that are planned far in advance, or are done over a long period of time, the solar year may be studied in the same manner as the lunar month. In other words, for increase you would work from Yule to Midsummer, building to the time of maximum daylight; and for decrease, work from Midsummer to Yule. Other aspects of the yearly cycle might be considered if you feel it necessary, including the time of planting, the time of harvest, pruning, birthing, and so on.

Putting It All Together

Let's look at an example to demonstrate what I've been talking about. Jane Smith and Frank Wilson are going into business together. They've invested their money in a small bookstore and want to do a ritual to ensure success when they open. (They are going to determine the exact opening date by astrology.) They will do a ritual which they have written themselves: TO ATTAIN SUCCESS IN A NEW ENDEAVOR.

What is the best day of the week to do this ritual? Monday is good for "merchandise," Wednesday for "business," Thursday for "desires," and Sunday for "hope" and "fortune." They need to determine which of these is the most important to them: Are they just out to make money, or do they want to sell a lot of books, and thereby educate and entertain many people? Do they, perhaps, hope for future expansion, and eventually to have a chain of bookstores? Assuming they're not in it just for the money, we'll rule out Sunday's "fortune." "Merchandise" and "business" similarly can be ignored, which leaves "hope" and "desire." Sunday is again ruled out because they want to do more than just *hope* for success—they *desire* it! Thursday would seem to be the day, then.

What is the best time of day? Now that they know it is their desire for success that's important (in all aspects of the business), they might choose Jupiter, since it is the planet of harmony, education, knowledge, and learning through reading. They might also choose Mercury—quick-witted, good for research, for writers, and for teachers. After carefully considering all aspects, Jane and Frank finally decide on Jupiter.

When in the month should they work? Obviously their best time is in the waxing phase of the moon, since they want to increase their business and move toward success. They should determine the date of the Full Moon, and make that the final day for their series of rituals. If they are doing just one ritual, then it should be done on the Full Moon.

When in the year should they work? The spring is the time for planting seeds; this, then, is the time for them to start working Magickally. They could do a series of rituals from the spring to culminate at Midsummer.

Now that they've decided on the general timing of their Magick, it's time to look at the calendar and pinpoint the actual days and hours. They know they're going to be starting their rituals in the spring, so they'll likely start on a Thursday in the waxing phase of the Moon. Looking at a calendar, Jane and Frank find that there's a New Moon on Sunday, April tenth.* They decide to start their ritual on the Thursday following that day, and work daily until the Full Moon on April twenty-fifth. They will then repeat the ritual on the first Thursday after the New Moon in May, and continue until the Full Moon in that month; and so on until Midsummer, June twenty-first. This falls just two days before a Full Moon, placing their rituals nicely within the waxing phase. (See Figure 1.)

Looking at the Planetary Hours for their start date, April fourteenth, Jane and Frank want to begin in the hour of Jupiter. On April fourteenth, sunrise is at 5:48 A.M., and sunset is at 6:11 P.M. That means that for daytime there are twelve sixty-two-minute "hours" (61.92 actually, but we'll round up), and for night there are twelve fifty-eight-minute "hours." On Thursday, Jupiter is the first hour of the day, and also the eighth. (See the Planetary Hours table.) This means that Jane and Frank can either do their ritual at 5:48 A.M. local time, or at 2:04 P.M. local time. (Eight times sixty-two equals 496 minutes after 5:48 A.M., which equals 2:04 P.M. actual time.)

---

*Spring comes at different times to different parts of the world. Choose an appropriate time for where you are. Don't forget that Daylight Savings Time may also be a factor.

April

S	M	T	W	Th	F	S
					1	2
3	4	5	6	7	8	9
NM 10	11	12	13	*14*	*15*	*16*
17	*18*	*19*	*20*	*21*	*22*	*23*
24	FM *25*	26	27	28	29	30

May

S	M	T	W	Th	F	S
1	2	3	4	5	6	7
8	NM 9	10	11	*12*	*13*	*14*
15	*16*	*17*	*18*	*19*	*20*	*21*
22	*23*	FM *24*	25	26	27	28
29	30	31				

June

S	M	T	W	Th	F	S
			1	2	3	4
5	6	7	NM 8	*9*	*10*	*11*
12	*13*	*14*	*15*	*16*	*17*	*18*
19	*20*	*21*	22	FM 23	24	25
26	27	28	29	30		

Figure 1. Jane and Frank's ritual performing schedule.

They could also do it during the night. Jupiter is the third and tenth hour in the night schedule. Counting from the start of the night "hours," 6:11 P.M., the third hour starts at 174 minutes (two hours and fifty-four minutes) after sunset, or at 9:05 P.M. actual local time. The tenth hour starts 580 minutes (nine hours and forty minutes) after sunset, or 3:51 A.M. local time on Friday morning. Although Friday morning technically falls into the twenty-four hour period of Thursday, we will discount it just to be on the safe side. This means that Jane and Frank have the choice of starting their ritual at 5:48 A.M., 2:04 P.M., or 9:05 P.M. on that Thursday.

It may seem to take a lot of mathematics to arrive at these times, but it's really not that difficult; just a matter of multiplying and dividing. Times will have to be worked out for every day the ritual is performed, of course.

Let's look at an another example. Jim Brown has been arguing with his teenage son and bickering with his wife for some time. He wants to settle down and bring peace and harmony back into the home. He found a ritual, TO SETTLE A DISTURBED CONDITION IN THE HOME, in my book, *Practical Candleburning Rituals* (Llewellyn, 1982). He would like to perform the Magick with as much going for him as he can possibly get. In other words, he wants to work an advanced version of that rite.

On what day should he start? The ritual has to be done on three consecutive days, but the starting day, as we've seen above, is the important one. Friday is a day for "love" and "friendship," and would seem to be the most appropriate. This means that he'll finish on a Sunday, which is also a day of hope, so that works out well.

At what time of day should he work the Magick? Pluto is associated with children and youth; Jupiter is the planet of harmony; the Moon is sensitive, emotional, and domestic; Venus, in addition to being the planet of love, also covers friendship and peacemaking. Jim chooses the hour of Venus for peacemaking.

He wants to get started right away, so there's no point to considering the time of year. It would, however, be good to work in the waxing phase of the moon, finishing as close to the Full Moon as possible. (As an alternative approach, Jim could work a different ritual to get rid of negativity in the house, which he would work in the waning cycle of the Moon.)

Let's say that it is approaching Yule—one reason why Jim finally wishes to address his family's situation. Looking at the calendar, Jim decides to start on Friday, December ninth, which is in the Moon's last quarter. On that day, sunrise is at 6:05 A.M., and sunset is at 4:59 P.M. This makes twelve daylight hours of 55 minutes each, and twelve nighttime hours of 65 minutes each. Venus is the first and eighth daytime hour, as well as the third and tenth night hour. (We'll ignore the tenth for the same reasons as in the above example.) The first hour of the day starts at 6:05 A.M. local time. The eighth is at eight times fifty-five—440 minutes, or seven hours and twenty minutes later. (6:05 plus 7:20 equals 13:25, or 1:25 P.M. local time.) With sunset at 4:59 P.M., and Venus at the third hour, the nighttime possibility is three times sixty-five (195 minutes), or three hours and fifteen minutes after sunset. This would be 4:49 P.M. plus 3:15, or 8:04 P.M. local time. Jim has a choice of working at 6:05 A.M., 1:25 P.M., or 8:04 P.M. on the first day of the ritual. By the same method, Jim works out the times for Saturday (with Venus the fifth and twelfth daylight hours, and the seventh nighttime hour) as 10:40 A.M., 5:05 P.M., and 12:34 A.M. (Sunday morning). For Sunday (second and ninth daylight; fourth and eleventh nighttime) the hours are 7:55 A.M., 2:20 P.M., and 9:19 P.M.

With a little bit of math it is possible to find the absolute best time to work your rituals. Not only that, but you get a choice of times!

V

PREPARATION FOR
RITUAL WORKING

Certain tools are necessary for performing Magick, but is it also important how you dress? Most people do candleburning in their everyday clothes, and enjoy a fair degree of success; but would they have even greater success if they paid special attention to what they wore? I think they would. To prepare your body and to put on special clothing, *used only when working Magick*, helps place your mind in a special state which can only be a stimulus to the Magick itself.

Many Magicians around the world, in primitive societies and sophisticated ones, are naked when they perform their Magick. Many Wiccan traditions work this way, for example. At first glance being naked would seem to be the antithesis of "dressing up" to do ritual work. Yet to go through the process of removing all

clothing just to do Magick can be as emotionally charging as putting on special clothes. Being naked for the
rites is, therefore, one possibility.

Before we get further into the appropriateness of
clothing, let's consider the state of the body. How should
we prepare that?

Preparing the Body

For any Magickal operation it is best to be at the peak of
physical fitness. To quote from my book, *Buckland's Complete Book of Witchcraft* (Llewellyn Publications, 1986),

> To be able to produce power we must be in good
> shape. A sick tree bears little fruit. Keep yourself in
> good physical condition. You don't have to run five
> or ten miles a day, or have to lift weights to do this.
> Just see to it that you do not get grossly overweight
> (or underweight, for that matter). Watch your diet.
> Cut down on the junk food and try to keep a balanced
> diet; though what is balanced for one person may
> not be so for another. Try to stick to natural foods.
> Avoid sugar (aptly known as "the white death"!) and
> bleached flour. Eat plenty of vegetables and fruit.
> I don't suggest you become a vegetarian, but don't
> overindulge in (red) meat. You'll know if you are in
> good shape because you'll feel good.
>
> Cleanliness, before working Magick, is important. It is
> good practice to cleanse the inner body by fasting. Eat

and drink nothing but water, honey and whole wheat bread for twenty-four hours beforehand. No alcohol or nicotine; no sexual activity.... Before the ritual, bathe in water to which has been added a tablespoonful of salt; preferably sea salt (this can be purchased at most supermarkets or at health food stores).

A ritual bath is a necessity before starting any Magickal rite. This is not a physical cleansing bath with lots of soap, although if one is needed by all means indulge before the ritual bath! The ritual bath is simply a submersion into a bath of fresh, clean water to which has been added special salts, oils, or herbs. It's an attunement of the body; the vibrations of the treated water blend with the physical form to reach a level of harmony. As mentioned, sea salt is the basic additive, and will always suffice if nothing else is available. Where possible, use bath salts or herbs prescribed for the particular ritual.

For herb baths, gather a small bunch of the herb(s) and tie them in a small muslin or cheesecloth bag. Steep this in a bowl of hot (not boiling) water for a few minutes, then add that charged water to the bath water just before you get in. (You can also transfer the bag of herbs to the bath itself, if you wish.) While soaking in the water, center your thoughts on the object of the ritual which lies ahead. The bath is a *ritual* bath. In other words, the bath is a part of your ritual. That being the case, the time to do your protective light-building is just before you step into the bath. (See Chapter Six.)

Oils

Oils are used in many ways: to dress the candles (more on this later), in the ritual bath instead of herbs or salts, and directly on the body. The process of making true essential oils is long, painstaking, and can be quite expensive. For this reason here is one place where I do advise you to purchase the ingredients. Many New Age, natural food, and metaphysical stores sell oils. There are also many catalog companies which offer them. If you are to blend two or more oils, be careful to do it with oils from the same source. Do not try to blend synthetic oils that have come from two different places; frequently they are incompatible (due to the cutting agents used, etc.). When you do blend oils, use a long-necked, round-based, glass container. Pour them in slowly and gently swirl the container clockwise. Do not shake or stir. Oils are very subtle and need careful handling.

When using oils, measure them with an eyedropper, using a separate eyedropper for each so as not to pollute. Store them away from heat and light.

Bath Salts

As with all things Magickal, it is best to make your own bath salts, and this is easy to do. The three main ingredients are: table salt (or better yet, sea salt), Epsom salts, and baking soda (sodium bicarbonate). These can be mixed in a variety of proportions, but equal parts do fine. Be sure to mix thoroughly. Color and oils can also be added to your salts as desired. For color, use food coloring; and, if you are using a combination of colors, premix in a small bowl and add slowly, drop by drop, to the bath salts. Similarly, the essential oils should be added very slowly, carefully blending them with the salts. While mixing your bath salts, concentrate on the purpose of the salts and the ritual.

Crystals and Stones

Occasionally I recommend using a particular crystal (precious or semi-precious stone) as an amplifier in a ritual. This is exactly what these stones are: amplifiers. A crystal will magnify the Magickal energies at work. If you are able, use the stones recommended for your ritual. If not, either use a plain, white quartz crystal, or dispense with that part of the ritual altogether. Do not try to substitute say, jade for emerald or garnet for ruby. Color is important, but in this case it is the qualities of the particular stone which are being called upon—not just the color. (See Table 8, "Properties of Precious and Semi-Precious Stones," in the Appendix.)

Magickal Tool Construction

Constructing Magickal tools—including robes, which are certainly tools—is a very important part of working

Magick. It is fairly easy to find just about any tool offered for sale these days. Many stores and catalog houses specialize in Magickal items; but no matter how slick and glossy, how "professional" the appearance of the bought item, it in no way compares, Magickally, to the simple crude-looking object you make yourself. Even a tool said to be "made by a genuine Magician/ Witch/ Magickal Craftsman" is not as good for your purposes as one you create. Why is that? It's because of the energy, the "power," you put into the tool as you make it. If you craft the tool, it's *your* power that's going into it. If someone else makes the tool, no matter their claims, who knows what's in there!

The secret of making effective tools is concentration. That sounds easy, but it's not. You need to be concentrating on the *purpose* of the tool *the whole time you are making it.* (More on this in Chapter Nine.)

Robes

I think Magickal robes are an excellent idea. First of all, wearing them strictly for your Magickal work puts you into a certain state of mind which helps empower you. More than that, the actual making of the robes is part of the Magick.

What you wear does not have to be of any special type or style, but long, flowing sleeves can be a hazard when draping over lit candles; so do, please, be safety minded.

I'm using the word "robe," but this can apply to anything you decide to wear while working Magick. It can be the traditional long robe of the ceremonial Magician, or it can be a simple pair of pants, or skirt and top. It must, however, be something that you have made for this purpose only, and that is worn for this purpose only. It is *special*, and by virtue of that, it is Magickal.

In *Buckland's Complete Book of Witchcraft* I give details on making a robe. The "CM Robe" described in my *Practical Color Magick* could be ideal. What color robe would be best for you? My personal favorite is a deep green. It is a color of nature, but more than that, or perhaps because of it, it is a soothing, relaxing color for me. You choose what is right for you. (See Figure 2.)

Of course, you can make more than one robe, each in a different color, if you wish; but here I'd advise caution: you don't want to spread your energies too thinly to start. Better to decide on one color (or combination of colors), and work with that for a while. This way you can put all your energy into making that one robe. White, which is actually a combination of all colors, is a good choice. Black, which is the absence of color, is probably a poor choice.

As with color, the material you use is up to you. I would suggest a natural material, such as cotton, linen, or silk, rather than a polyester or nylon, but again, it's what makes you most comfortable that's important.

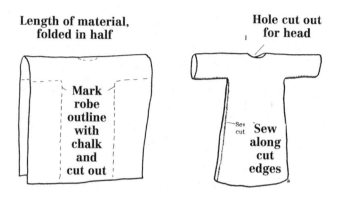

Figure 2. A simple robe.

As you lay out your robe, as you cut it and as you sew it (traditionally it is sewn by hand, not on a machine) concentrate on the fact that this is the garment you are going to wear when you work your candle Magick. This is a Magickal garment! Think about that. Put your power and your energy into every stitch. Know that when you put on this robe you are going to feel energy pulsating through your body. It is going to be a part of you and will add to your Magickal power. If you want to decorate it, you can sew, appliqué, or paint onto the robe.

When the robe is completed, wrap it carefully in a white cloth and put it away where you plan to store your Magickal paraphernalia.

Wand

A wand is an optional tool. Some people like to use one; others do not. Magick wands, in one form or another, are found going back to earliest times in all civilizations. They are not only a symbol of power, but also a very real means of administering that power. Shamans, Amerindian medicine men, obeah men of Africa, ancient Egyptians, Druids, priests, rulers, and wisemen have all borne the Magickal staff or scepter which is the wand of power.

The purpose of a wand is to store and project your power. You can store the energy in your body and project it with your finger if you prefer, however, for many people the use of a wand is a means of focusing; of mentally balancing the forces. It certainly can be a psychologically worthwhile tool.

The material you use is optional. If you can work in metal, then a copper, brass, or silver wand is not out of the question. For most people, a wooden wand is best; and wood is traditional because of its properties, or "vibrations." I feel it is most appropriate. Here again, the type of wood is up to you. Hazel wood was a favorite of magicians of old, though the Druids preferred yew, rowan, or hawthorn. Soft woods, such as pine, cedar, and spruce, are easiest to work with, especially if you are planning on carving the wand. (See Figure 3.) Hard woods, such as oak, hickory, and mahogany, are more difficult to work with.

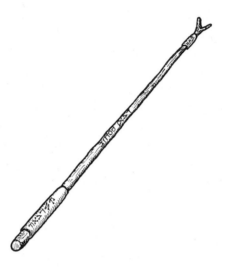

Figure 3. Wand.

A traditional length for a wand is the distance from your longest fingertip to your elbow. Other "traditional" lengths are eighteen inches or twenty-one inches. Thickness is about that of a finger or thumb. You could use a length of dowel for a wand, although most wands taper toward the tip. Also, it's nice to go out and cut your own piece of wood. Look for a fallen tree when you do this, though; and always thank the tree and the nature spirits for what they have given you.

Whether you leave the bark on the wood or strip it off is up to you. You can also polish, oil, paint, or varnish it, if you so desire. The handle can be simple or it can be bound with cloth, leather, or copper wire. You could also leave the bark on at the handle, and strip it off for the rest of the length. Some people like to add a crystal, or crystals, to the wand. I don't think it's necessary, although I do like a tip bound with a piece of silver or copper. Designs can be carved along the wand's length, or woodburned or painted on. All this decoration is a matter of personal taste. The main thing is, you should *have a reason for everything you do.* Don't just stick a double-terminated quartz crystal on the tip, burn an assortment of Germanic runes along its length, and wind purple cloth about the handle because you think it looks great; do it because you feel the crystal will amplify the energies, the runes have significance in your heritage, and the purple is your personal power color. In other words, have a reason—a good reason—for anything and everything you do to the wand. This applies to all your tools. It is important to do *something* to the wand, even if it's only shaping it, because in working on it you are imbuing it with your energies. As you are making it, don't forget to concentrate on the Magickal uses to which you will put the wand.

Awl

You will have to mark the candles with names or properties for some of the rituals. To do this you will use an awl, or engraver. This is a small tool, about the size of a pen or pencil. In fact it's used in similar fashion to a

Figure 4. Awl.

pen, but scratches, or engraves, the characters into the wax of the candles. For this reason the point does not have to be especially sharp; a fine, but nicely rounded point is best. (See Figure 4.)

One way to make an awl is to find a piece of wood (you could get it at the same time you get your wood for the wand), and carve it into shape. Take a small nail (a 4-D would do) and tap it firmly into the end of the wood, being careful not to split the wood. With a pair of sidecutters, cut off the head of the nail, and then sharpen the end on a grindwheel. If you don't have a grindwheel you can put a point on it by working it against a rough stone. In fact, this might be the preferable method, since in Magick you are not trying to do things the quick and easy way, you are working at putting your energies into your tools. As an alternative, you can use a hard wood and just sharpen the end, leaving the nail out. It would certainly do the job of engraving in candle wax. You may decorate the awl with pertinent symbols and colors, but only if they are relevant to you.

Incense and Thurible

The burning of incense, or aromatic herbs, resins, and barks, at religious and other rites, is a practice of great antiquity found almost universally. It was an ancient belief that the smoke of incense carried one's prayers up to the gods. It is also a fact that incense-burning creates a certain atmosphere, or "vibes," which add immeasurably to a Magickal ritual.

Incense used in candleburning Magick is not especially esoteric, but it certainly has its place, and is yet another important ingredient to help achieve the ultimate Magickal power. Different incenses are recommended for different rituals; these are only suggestions, however. If you have a favorite, or are unable to obtain what is suggested, then go with what you've got or what you prefer. When a mixture of several incenses is suggested, do as we've been doing in preparing the other working tools: concentrate on the purpose of the ritual while mixing the incense. Put your thoughts and your power into the mixture so that, when it burns, it is focused on the ritual's purpose just as much as you are.

The ancient Egyptians often used what they called *kuphi.* This was an elaborate mixture of sixteen different ingredients. You won't need anything as complex as that, but on occasion you will be mixing two or three. In the rituals detailed in Part Three, the incense ingredients should be mixed in equal parts unless otherwise indicated.

Incense is burned on a charcoal briquette. This is not the type of charcoal briquette used on barbecues, which gives off poisonous fumes. *Do not use these.* The charcoal you will be using is available at metaphysical supply houses or religious supply stores. (Check the phone book.) These are self-lighting blocks, by which I mean they have saltpeter (potassium nitrate) mixed in so that a touch with a match will start them burning. After you have lit one of these blocks, it will sparkle for a moment as the saltpeter spreads the flame all over the surface. When it stops sparking, blow gently on it for a moment, just to be sure it's well and truly alight, then, with a spoon, drop just a very little incense onto it. One of the joys of this way of working is that it's very economical for your incense. Just add a little incense as you need it. There's no need to load it up.

Your thurible, or incense-burner, should ideally be one which can be swung on a chain. This swinging produces sufficient wind to keep the charcoal glowing. A wide variety of thuribles are available from many sources, but you can make your own, or modify an appropriate vessel. I have added a section of brass chain to one of those generally-available openwork brass boxes, made in India and sold at import stores, producing a very workable censer. A brass ashtray, drilled with some holes and hung on a chain, will also do the job. You can, if you have to, just place the charcoal on a dish or saucer, though first fill the dish with sand to absorb the heat and prevent cracking. This cannot be swung, but it can be picked up and waved through the air, which is acceptable.

Poppets

Some rituals call for the use of a poppet, or cloth figure made to represent a person and frequently used in sympathetic Magick. Specifics for making poppets are given in the rituals later in this book, but here are the basics.

The color of cloth used for the poppet is determined by the birth date of the person represented. For example, if the person is a Taurus then the poppet should be yellow, pink, or pale blue. If a Capricorn, blue, dark gray, or very dark green cloth should be used. (See Table 5, "Astral Colors," in the Appendix.) Cut out two shapes and sew them together, leaving just the top of the head open. (See Figure 5.) Concentrate on the person, or type of person the poppet represents, while cutting and sewing. To you, this crude figure *is that person*. You know that anything you should do to this figure, you will be doing to him or her! If this represents someone in particular, then it might help to have a photograph in front of you as you work, so you can really see the person in your mind's eye. (Revisit the ethics of

Magick discussed in Chapter One. This poppet must never be used to manipulate someone against his or her will. Always remember that.)

Now stuff the poppet with appropriate filling, which will depend upon the specific ritual. When in doubt, stuff it with calendula flowers or rose petals, then sew up the head. If known, necessary personal details can now be

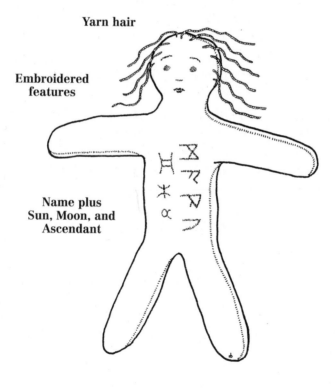

Yarn hair

Embroidered features

Name plus Sun, Moon, and Ascendant

Figure 5. Poppet.

added: yellow, brown, or black wool for the hair, facial hair drawn or embroidered on, colored eyes, etc. On the body the sun, moon, and rising signs can be painted or embroidered, if known. Even the name can be added, if appropriate. (See Table 13, "Magickal Alphabets," in the Appendix for forms of writing.) The poppet should be consecrated at the start of the ritual. Until then, wrap it in a clean white cloth and store it away.

Plackets

There will be occasions when you will use photographs, letters, and other objects in your rituals. If this is the case, they will be placed inside a small Magickal bag known as a placket (an old English word meaning "pocket" or "vagina"). You can make a number of these in advance. I would suggest making one in each of the

Figure 6. Placket with photograph.

primary colors—red, orange, yellow, green, blue, indigo, and violet. You may later need others with special combinations of colors (for example, red on one side and green on the other for healing), but you can do those when the time comes.

To make a placket, simply cut two rectangles out of felt, cotton, silk, or linen, and sew them together along three of the sides, leaving the fourth side open for inserting the photograph or letter. (See Figure 6.)

Talismans

Sometimes the use of a talisman in conjunction with candleburning can be helpful. A good example is when seeking protection while traveling. An easy yet powerful talisman is one of the "Magickal Squares." *The Book of Sacred Magic of Abra Melin the Mage* (translated by S. L. MacGregor Mathers) is probably the best known collection of these.

Magickal Squares consist of letters arranged to form a square. Numbers are also used, but we will confine our interest to letters. The letters are arranged to form various words of power, which are written forward and backward; downward and upward. There are traditional squares for such things as bringing money, health, protection, and love. The squares are drawn on parchment, using pen and ink (not a ball-point!). I would suggest drawing the lines of the squares in black ink, then writing in the letters with a color appropriate to the spell being done (for instance, green for money or red for love). For High Magick, the pen and ink each have to be made to a certain formula; but for candle Magick, you don't have to go to that much trouble. Any good-quality ink will do, together with a pen with a new nib. I would suggest India ink for the black, and a good artist's ink, such as Higgins or Pelikan, for the colors.

There are some important rules that should be followed when writing the letters or symbols:

1. All the letters and symbols should be the same size.

2. They must not touch the lines.

3. The symbols should be written in their sequence.

4. You should not allow your shadow to fall across the Square as you work on it. (Place the light source, or position yourself to the sun for this.)

5. You must concentrate on the purpose of the Square all the time you are constructing it. (In your mind, see the desire achieved.)

6. You should feel absolutely confident of the success you will achieve using the Square.

Having decided on the Magickal Square you will make, have the Magickal alphabets available, so the actual letters can be written in the characters of one of the alphabets. The Talisman must be constructed during the ritual. (See Part Three: "To Protect on a Journey," as an example.) Examples of Magickal Squares are in Table 9 in the Appendix.

Candles

The most important tools are the candles themselves; and because they are so important, and their preparation can be complex, I will devote an entire chapter to them. (See Chapter Seven.)

VI

YOUR MAGICKAL STUDY

C andleburning Magick can be done almost any-where, but here we're going the Rolls Royce route, so why not have your own private temple, Magickal study, sanctum, or whatever you want to call it? To have one special room just for working Magick is ideal. It's a quiet place where you know you will not be interrupted, and which you have specially prepared and consecrated for Magick.

Your room can be small. About ten feet square (one hundred square feet) is a good size. Many people convert attic or basement space by adding a wall or two, giving themselves Magickal space without encroaching on the rest of the house. If you are really pressed for space, perhaps living in an apartment, there are alternatives which I'll discuss below; but, for the moment, let's think in terms of a full room.

You should have a closet along one wall in which to store the items you are not currently using: your candles, incense and charcoal. Failing this, a large chest will do. Certain items you will probably leave on the altar permanently, while others will be there on a temporary basis, while being used.

Some people like to mark a circle on the floor, designating the actual ritual area. This is traditional, and any size circle that will comfortably hold you and the altar will suffice. I would suggest seven feet in diameter; seven being one of the Magickal numbers. This circle can be permanently marked or painted on the floor. Any additional markings are up to you. Some people write words and names of power around the circle (for instance, the names of angels and archangels, if you are of a Christian bent; or some of the names and words specified in books on ceremonial Magick). You might want to mark a large pentagram in the center, or have five-, six- or seven-pointed stars around the edge. None of this is mandatory, but if it gives you added comfort, why not?

Having drawn your circle, it is a good idea to consecrate it to make this a "special," if not holy, space. By doing so, you will protect yourself from unwanted psychic phenomena. Let me say here that there is no need to become paranoid about "psychic attack," or fear evil entities being drawn in! First of all, there is an ancient occult law that says, "like attracts like." If you are the sort of person who goes around kicking small animals and tripping old ladies then yes, you might attract something unpleasant; but if you are the average good person, striving to live a clean life, you are not going to be attracting anything negative. I will give you a short psychic exercise which should be done before starting any psychic work such as candle Magick. This will keep you safe and sound while you are working.

Consecrating Your Circle

Stand at one point just inside the line of the circle. Traditionally one starts in the east, but this is not mandatory for this type of Magick. Take a few deep breaths and imagine your body filling with light. As you breathe in, see and feel the light entering your body and pushing out any aches, pains, or negativity. It helps to think of this cleansing light as coming from somewhere. Some see it coming down from the sky (perhaps from the gods), and entering at the position of the third eye (between and slightly above the point where the eyebrows would meet). Others, myself included, imagine it coming up through the soles of the feet, being drawn from the earth itself. Even if you are in a high-rise apartment, you can imagine this energy coming from Mother Earth, working its way up through the building, finally finding and entering you. See and feel this light as a very positive force, filling you with goodness, energy, and power. You can see it as white light, gold, blue, or any color you choose.

Now point the forefinger of your right hand (left, if left-handed) at your circle, and imagine the energy within your body moving along your arm, off the end of your finger, and down like a projected light into the circle. Walk slowly around the circle clockwise, directing this energy into the circle, until you return to the spot where you started. Then move into the center of the circle and stand quietly for a moment. Continue to breathe deeply and to draw in the light, but now see that light filling your body and expanding in all directions. See it slowly spreading until it meets and blends with the light-energy you have used to mark the circle. You are now completely encased in this positive light. Your Magickal area is consecrated and ready for use.

I spoke of a short psychic exercise you can do before starting any psychic work. This is really a renewal—a re-charging—of what you have just done. Before the start of any candle Magick ritual, stand or kneel in the center of your circle and, closing your eyes, draw once again on that light and energy, filling your body with it. Breathe it in and breathe out all the negativity. There is no need to redo the walking and charging of the circle, that is now consecrated space; but as you refill your body at the start of each ritual, it will meld and blend with that space, keeping you safe and sound. This is creating your sacred space.

The Altar

You will need an altar in the circle. This should be placed in half of the space, leaving you room to stand and move in the other half. You can use an old wooden chest, a small table, or even a small chest of drawers. Ideally you might make an altar especially for your Magickal study. *Buckland's Complete Book of Witchcraft* contains plans for building one, although you can probably make a simple one even without plans. The top surface should be twenty-two by thirty inches or thereabouts, and of a height to suit you.

Some people paint their altar, others varnish it or leave the wood bare. Some place an altar cloth on it and others do not. I think altar cloths can be nice, since they give you a chance to be creative with simple border decorations. They also allow you to use different colors according to the purpose of the ritual (for example, a green cloth when doing money Magick, or pink for love).

A Closet Study

What about people who do not live in a house, but in a small apartment or condominium? Where can they find room for a special Magickal study?

I've known resourceful people who have taken over a large closet. This might be a problem if you have any claustrophobic tendencies, but even then it's possible to place your altar in one end of a closet and leave room at the other end for you to sit, stand, or kneel, with the door open. (See Figure 7.) The altar in this arrangement can also be the storage chest or chest of drawers. You can even put a lock on the door of the closet, if you have any sort of problems with a roommate, for instance.

In such a set-up there is no room to draw a circle around everything; this just means that you must be sure to do the exercise to create your sacred space at the start of every ritual. When you have filled your body with the light, simply continue breathing it in and see it expanding to fill the whole closet. Do this every time you use the space.

If your living conditions are such that you cannot even manage a closet for your Magickal study, then you will have to make do with the corner of a room, or with a temporary altar as described in *Practical Candleburning Rituals*.

Figure 7. A closet candleburning study.

VII

MAKING CANDLES FOR CANDLE MAGICK

The most important tools in candle Magick are, of course, the candles themselves. While it is possible to simply buy various colored candles, it is far more satisfactory, not to mention Magickally empowering, to make your own.

A wide variety of candles are used in Magick: image candles, treasure candles, knob candles, jar candles, dipped, molded, beeswax, and sand-cast. As with any of the other tools, making the candles is as much a part of the ritual as is burning them on the altar. Let's start by looking at basic, colored candles.

Types of Magickal Candles

As was pointed out at the beginning of the book, Magick is not necessarily connected with religion. You can be an agnostic or even an atheist and still practice Magick; but some people do like to tie in their beliefs in deity with their Magickal workings. For these people, one or two ALTAR CANDLES are appropriate. These are usually tall, white candles, placed on the back of the altar, and lit before any of the others. For those with a belief in male and female deities, using two image candles for the Altar Candles can work well.

OFFERTORY CANDLES come in various colors which represent different things depending upon the work being done. For example, orange is the color of attraction. Therefore, if you are trying to attract something to you, you would place an orange candle beside the candle representing yourself. Green is the color for money, so a green candle would be used to represent wealth in a ritual. (For a list of the colors and what they symbolize, see Table 4, "Symbolism of Colors," in the Appendix. Note: Different systems have different color symbolism. The Appendix also includes color symbolisms for Native American and Asian systems. If these, or other systems, are closer to your heart, then go with what is right for you; but, as in all things Magickal, be consistent.)

ASTRAL CANDLES represent the people involved in the ritual. The PETITIONER is the person who is working the Magick, either you or the person on whose behalf you are working. The other Astral Candles are the other people involved. The color of these candles is chosen depending upon the birthdate of the person. For example, a person born on August fifth is under the astrological sign of Leo, and so a red, or combination red-and-green candle would be used. Each sign has both Primary and Secondary colors. *Whenever possible both colors should be used.* This helps differentiate an Astral Candle from an Offertory Candle, among other things. (See Table 5, "Astral Colors," in the Appendix).

Which DAY CANDLES are burned depends upon the day on which the ritual is being done. For example, if it's a ritual being done on a Friday, then a Green candle would be burned. Offertory, Astral, and Day candles should be dipped-taper or rolled-beeswax candles. It is suggested that Astral Candles be made slightly taller than Offertory and Day Candles.

Candlemaking Basics

Do not take shortcuts when making candles for Magickal purposes. Don't use second-hand wax, collected from already burned candles, or ordinary cord in place of proper wicking. Pioneers used wicks made of rolled cotton, silky down from milkweeds, cattail stems, or tow string; but correct wicking is important to good burning. Wick sizes are labeled according to the number of threads plaited together. For a candle one to three inches in diameter, a fifteen-ply wick should be used. For a four-inch-diameter candle, use a twenty-four-ply wick, and for over four inches, use a thirty-ply wick.

Most waxes used in candles today are a blend of paraffin and stearine, or stearic acid. Church candles are made of forty-eight percent paraffin and fifty-two percent beeswax, while ordinary candles are seventy percent paraffin, twenty percent stearic acid, and ten percent beeswax (or ninety percent paraffin and ten percent stearic acid). If you can get the wax used for church candles, do so.

Wax is best melted in a double-boiler or in an electric crockpot (never use a glass container). Most waxes melt between 110°F and 200°F (the boiling point of water is 213°F). Beeswax melts at 144°F to 147°F. Be very careful not to melt wax in a pot over an open flame, since the flames can leap up the side of the pot and ignite the wax. Use a double-boiler or a crockpot for safety. If you *should* have a flame-up, smother it with baking soda (keep an open box handy) and *not* with water.

It helps to have a thermometer to keep an eye on the temperature. Get one of the all-metal rod thermometers with a dial on the top. These are available from laboratory supply houses. With this type, you can also use the stem of the thermometer for stirring the wax. (Caution: Overheated wax can produce a toxic byproduct called acrolein, which can damage the *medulla oblongata* area of the brain. *Use proper ventilation at all times* when making candles.)

Both wax and wicking can be purchased from local handicraft stores, or from national wholesalers. Go to your local library and check the Yellow Pages for New York, Chicago, Los Angeles, and other large cities to find suppliers. (I find that if I include names and addresses in a book such as this, the companies relocate or go out of business, so that there is the constant need to update. Far better that you track them down yourself.) You might also check handicraft magazines, which sometimes list current suppliers.

Coloring Candles

Never use water-based or food coloring to color your candles. If you are seriously into candle making, use powdered color, an oil-soluble aniline dye, or natural colors. Some people use things such as wax crayons, Tintex or Rit dyes, and powdered paints. Probably the wax crayons are the easiest, but they are far from the best. The main problem with crayons is that there can be a chemical reaction whereby the wick gets eaten away. Dyes frequently color unevenly. You really want wax-soluble dyes. Check with hobby shops for candle-coloring agents, especially powdered colors, which are best for your purposes. Remember that most wax color gets lighter as it hardens, so experiment with how much to use.

You can use natural dyes to color candles, and this is strongly recommended. Except when dyeing with indigo, the basic method is simply to put the dye (blossom, leaves) in a nylon bag and add it to the melted wax. The foot of a pair of panty-hose makes an ideal bag for this. Most fresh plant material will color the wax sufficiently in about an hour. If it isn't dark enough by that time, remove the bag and replace it with a second one of fresh plant. Keep heating the wax with the bag of herbs in it until the color is right for you. If you get the color too dark, simply add more wax to lighten it.

When dyeing with indigo, add stearic acid to the hot wax first, followed by a small muslin bag containing about a tablespoonful of indigo powder. The stearic acid is necessary to extract the color.

Jo Lohmolder,* an expert chandler, suggests the following proportions of plant material per pound of wax:

Fresh leaves or blossoms: 2 cups pressed down

Fresh (green) black walnut or butternut hulls: 1/2 cup

Lichens: 1/4 cup

Osage orange root: 1/2 cup (of the papery outer covering)

She has also compiled a table of natural materials to use. (See Figure 8.)

---

* *The Herb Companion* magazine, October/November 1989.

Color	Plant	Part used
Beige	Silver Queen Armetisia	All parts
Rosy Beige	Bloodroot Prickly Ash	Root Unripe berries
Blue	Indigo	Powder
Deep Brown	Butternut	Green husks
Gold	Oxeye Daisy Lichens Catfoot Everlasting	Blossoms All Leaves and blossoms
Brassy Gold	Black Walnut	Green husks
Old Gold	Black-eyed Susan	Blossoms
Gray	Lichen	All
Green	Tansy	Leaves
Gray-Green	Ambrosia Bayberry	Blossoms Berries
Olive-Green	Garden Sage Rosemary	Blossoms Leaves
Orange	Osage Orange	Papery root covering
Golden Orange	Myrrh	All
Pink	Cochineal	Powder
Rose	Cochineal	Powder
Yellow	Lichen	All
Golden Yellow	African Marigold	Blossoms

Figure 8. Natural materials for coloring wax.

Dipped Tapers

In this method, a length of wick is repeatedly dipped into hot wax until there is sufficient build-up to make a candle.

Obtain or make a metal can greater in length than the candle you are going to make. A three-pound coffee can is good (though these days it's actually two pounds, seven ounces!), rendering a candle up to six and one-half inches in length. A black iron can is best. Avoid copper, since it darkens the color of the wax, and gives it a burnt odor. Melt wax in the can until it is as full as the length of candle you require plus about one inch.

The smaller size plaited wicks, such as fifteen ply, are best for making taper candles. Cut the wick to suitable length and fasten a small nut or heavy washer to the end to weight it and keep it straight. To make two or three candles at once, you can make a line of these wicks on a length of wood. (See Figure 9.) A dowel is good for this, and notching the dowel keeps the wicks where you want them.

If the dip time is too short, and the wax temperature too low, you'll get a lumpy surface and poor adhesion. Conversely, if the temperature is too high, and the dip time too long, you'll get thinner layers, and it will take a longer time than necessary. Also, if you hold the wick in the wax too long, you'll start to melt the hardened wax from the previous dips. A 130°F melting-point wax brought to a temperature of 160°F, dipping for three to five seconds with two to three minutes between dips,

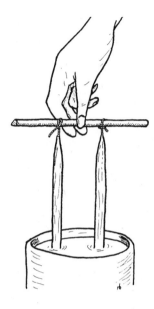

Figure 9. Dipping candles.

and with an outside air temperature (for cooling) of about 75°F, are the best conditions.

The steps to making a really good dipped candle are as follows:

1. Dip the wick into the wax and hold it for about three minutes the first time. This will remove air and moisture.

2. Bring it out and, as it cools, smooth it between your fingers, getting rid of any rough, bubbly areas. One way to do this is to roll it on a warm sheet of glass.

3. Dip again, but only up to one-quarter of its length. Hold for three to five seconds.

4. Withdraw for three minutes.

5. Dip up to half of its length, for three to five seconds.

6. Withdraw for three minutes.

7. Dip up to three-quarters of its length for three to five seconds.

8. Withdraw for three minutes.

9. Dip fully and withdraw.

10. Dip to one-third of its length and withdraw.

11. Dip to two-thirds of its length and withdraw.

12. Dip fully and withdraw.

13. Continue fully dipping and withdrawing until you reach desired diameter.

With a number of wicks on a length of wood, you can dip one, then move on to the second, then the third, and so on. By the time you've dipped them all, it will be almost time to start over with the second dip. In this way, with dips of different lengths, you get a good taper effect. If you really go into production, you can dip four to six wicks at a time (in a larger diameter can), and have the sets suspended from the spokes of a wheel, or something similar. You then rotate the wheel, bringing the can of wax up to the wicks, rather than taking the wicks down to the wax. You will need to keep an eye on the amount of wax in the can, and have more ready, at the right temperature, so that you can top off the can as the level drops.

Don't get too much into the production aspect, though. It's fine just for making candles, but you are creating Magickal tools, each one worthy of your special attention. Not only that, but you need to be concentrating on the purpose of each candle with every dip. For example, if you are dipping light-blue candles, think of tranquillity, understanding, patience, and health as you are dipping. Don't just think about it, but visualize those properties going into the candle as it builds. *Know* that the candle possesses those properties!

Two-Color Candles

For the Astral Candles, which are two colors, you will need dipping cans of both colors available. Let's use Taurus as an example. Red is the primary color and yellow the secondary.

Do the initial wick-soaking dip in the red, and then the next four dips (steps three, five, seven, and nine) also in the red. The next three dips (ten, eleven, and twelve) should be in the yellow. Then do a couple of full dips in the red (or three or four, depending upon how thick you want it), and two final dips, *covering only the lower half of the candle*, in the yellow. You will then have a candle where the majority of it is red, and the minority yellow, showing red on the top half and yellow on the lower half.

Another method is to take three thin-dipped tapers—two of the primary color and one of the secondary—and plait them together while still soft; or just use two colors and twist them together. With dipping, plaiting, or twisting Astral Candles, you can concentrate on the attributes of the particular astrological sign, if you are familiar with astrology. If not, don't worry about it, because you will later be personalizing that candle, anyway.

Rolled Beeswax Candles

These are the easiest candles to make. You can get beeswax in assorted, colored honeycomb sheets. All you do is lay the wick along the length at the edge, and tightly roll the sheet into a cylinder. When you lay down the wick, fold the edge of the honeycomb sheet over it, and crimp it down tightly, so that it makes a snug fit. Roll tightly. Usually three sheets are used for one candle, overlapping each into the rolling fold of the previous one. If you are making Astral Candles, you can use the primary color for the inner and outer sheets, and the secondary color for the middle sheet. Once again, concentrate your thoughts as you roll these candles.

Molding Candles

Molding, or casting, is good for Offertory and Day Candles. You can buy commercial molds, or you can make your own from tin, pewter, glass, plaster, rubber, or plastic; in fact, almost anything that won't melt and that will allow the release of the candle after it cools will do. You can use cardboard tubes (ex-toilet-paper or paper-towel tubes), milk cartons, wood, sand, clay, or tin cans.

Think of the purpose of the candle when considering the mold you'll use. For the Day Candles, the molds can be either quite small (egg shells, for example, or polyethylene-coated paper cups), or quite large, so that they can be used many times (paperboard milk cartons, perhaps). The Offertory Candles should be special, although you can still be creative. They could be molded in a cone shape, for example, or pyramidal.

Open-ended molds are perhaps the easiest to use. You will need a baseboard (with a small hole in the middle) on which to stand the mold, and a cross-piece to hang the wick. There should be a means to fasten the cross-piece securely to the wooden base on which the mold sits. (See Figure 10.) The mold itself can be cylindrical, corrugated, hexagonal, octagonal, or whatever. The sides can be parallel or tapered, as in a cone or pyramid. Release of the candle from the mold is most important, so remember that some material, such as paper or cardboard, may be of use only once.

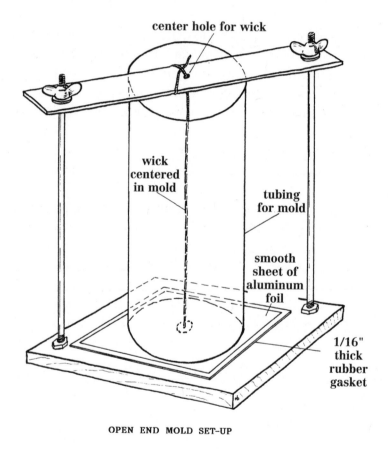

OPEN END MOLD SET-UP

Figure 10. Open-end mold set up.

Prewax a suitable length of wick by dipping it into hot wax for about a minute. Remove it, wipe it with a paper towel, and allow it to cool, keeping it as straight as possible. Tie a small knot in one end. Thread the open end of the wick through the hole in the baseboard, and up through a rubber gasket and aluminum foil. Take the wick up through the mold (you can probably do this best by holding everything upside down and letting the free end of the wick fall through the mold). Then take the free end through the hole in the cross-piece of wood, which you rest on top of the mold. The knot at the bottom, below the baseboard, will keep the wick from pulling up.

Make sure the mold is centered over the aluminum foil. Fasten the two end bolts that hold the cross-piece firm, and which also press the mold down against the aluminum and the rubber gasket, sealing the bottom of the mold. Finally, tie the top of the wick firmly around the cross-piece. You are now ready to pour your mold.

Pour in the wax at a high enough temperature to allow good mold formation and air bubble release before the wax cools. Pour in just a small amount to start, let it set up, and then slowly pour in the rest. Let it sit for about half an hour, and then top it off if there has been any contraction. After about four hours you can check to see if there are any obvious cavities around the wick area. Puncture the top surface with a stick or a pencil to open up the candle, getting rid of air pockets. Top it off again with hot wax. Let it stand for another eight hours. Do not attempt to release the candle from the mold until the wax has cooled *completely*. (This could be as long as twenty-four hours.)

To release the mold, undo the bolts holding the cross-piece, and untie the wick. Remove the cross-piece. Cut off the knot at the bottom of the baseboard and remove the board, aluminum foil, and rubber gasket. That end is actually going to be the *top* of your finished candle. The candle is released by tapping the mold sharply on a solid wooden surface. If it refuses to release, place the mold and candle in the refrigerator for about an hour. This will shrink the candle enough to release it. Cut off the wick that was tied around the cross-piece flush with that end of the candle. That is the base. Let the finished candle sit for four or five days.

You can coat some mold materials with oil or silicone ahead of time to facilitate the removal of the finished candle. Just wipe a very fine film of oil on the mold's inner surface, because any excess will cause bubbles to form in the wax.

Sand Molds

It is possible to use wet sand as your mold, and cast very interesting candles. Sand has the advantage that it can be scooped into virtually any shape and size you desire. The finished candle can then be dug quite easily out of the mold. You can press various shaped glasses, vases, seashells, pieces of wood or metal, or any other form into the wet sand to make the mold shape, or you can just press it out with your fingers.

You can make a simple sand mold by lining a cardboard box with a plastic bag and filling it with sand. You can also put the sand in an old cooking pot or large tin can. Add water in the proportion of approximately one gallon to fifty pounds of sand. Water does tend to settle to the bottom, so make sure it is well mixed. You'll find that the higher the temperature of the wax when you pour it, and the drier the sand, the more the wax will penetrate the sand, and the thicker the sand wall will be on the finished candle. The best temperature for the wax is about 250°F, and certainly not above 300°F.

Ladle the wax into the mold, being careful not to disturb the sand more than can be helped (pouring tends to be too disruptive). Use a straight piece of metal-core wick, crimped into a wick tin at the bottom. Place it in the center of your mold and support it until the wax solidifies. When the candle has completely set, carefully scoop away the sand around it, lift out the candle, and brush off any surplus sand. As with all of the above methods, it is imperative to concentrate on the purpose of the candle while making it.

Image Candles

It is possible to buy molds for making image candles—
candles shaped like a man or a woman. Such candles
can be very useful if only in helping you visualize who
it is they represent. By buying one of these molds, and
then making the candle to the prescribed astral colors
for the person while concentrating on that person, you
can produce a very powerful Astral Candle. If you happen to have something belonging to the person, such
as a few hairs or nail clippings, you can blend these
in with the wax as you fill the mold. (You can do the
same with regular straight molds.) Another strong way
to personalize an image candle is to take a photograph
of the person and chop it up into tiny pieces which can
be embedded in the candle as you mold it. (See "Additives," below, for more on this.)

Jar Candles

If you have an on-going ritual—let's say one for main-
taining a loving marriage—then you might want to place
your main candles, those of the people involved, inside
jars. You can buy special candle jars, but ordinary can-
ning jars will do. When you have completed your ritual,
you can then keep the jar(s) either on a shelf or in a
safe place, as a constant reminder of the purpose of the
ritual.

The jar candle is actually one of the simplest to make. Metal core wicking, which is fairly rigid, should be used. Its end is crimped into a small metal plate so that it will sit in the bottom center of the jar. Some sort of clip, such as a straightened paper-clip, will secure the wick in the center of the glass at the top. (See Figure 11.) Pour about a half-inch of wax into the jar and allow it to solidify. Check the straightness and centering of the wick, then pour in more wax to fill the jar within a half-inch of the top. Allow the wax to solidify. When it's ready, check the area around the wick to make sure there are no cavities or air pockets. Top off with more wax if necessary. When all is set, remove the clip at the top, and trim the wick to a desirable length (about one-half to three-quarters of an inch above the top of the candle).

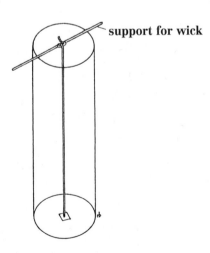

support for wick

Figure 11. Jar candle.

You can also make seven-day votive lights this way. For these there is a choice of jars: short, tall, flared, tapered, square shouldered, etc. Whichever you choose, be sure to use a metal-core wick.

A good way to make a two-colored jar candle is to first make a molded candle in one color, as described above, of a diameter less than that of the jar to be used. When fully set, place that candle in the middle of the jar and pour in the second color wax to fill the jar. (See Figure 12.)

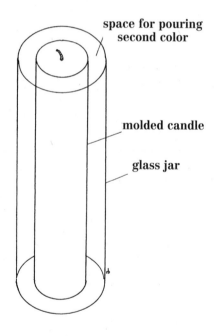

Figure 12. Two-color jar candle.

Special Purpose Jar Candles

You can also make special purpose jar candles. For example, a jar candle to attract money. Without the whole altar set up or any other candles, you can burn the jar candle continuously, and it will constantly attract money. To any outsider's eyes it is simply an attractive candle burning in your home. To house the candle, you can use any decorative jar, a fancy tumbler, or even a brandy snifter. You can make one to bring love, health, or anything you like. (See also "Additives" below.)

Knotted Wick Candles

These can work like seven-day candles, but with extra power. First take your wick and, after doing your psychic light-building exercise, mentally focus on the purpose for which the candle will be used. Let's use overcoming a bad habit as an example. Perhaps you're trying to give up smoking and plan a candleburning ritual to do it. Let's say you smoke a pack a day; that's twenty cigarettes a day, or 140 a week. You plan to stop smoking over a period of one week.

Mentally focus on your smoking as you hold the wick in your hand. See yourself cutting down from 140 cigarettes a week to 120 a week. Really see yourself having cut out that extra pack over the week's period.

Feel yourself feeling very much better for it; breathing easier and being happier. Concentrate hard on it and tie a knot in the wick.

Then do the same thing, but see yourself cutting down to one hundred cigarettes a week. Again feel good about it. Really put everything into it, and again tie a knot in the wick. Keep going like this: cutting to eighty a week, then sixty, then forty, twenty, and finally no cigarettes at all. Each time tie a knot until you have seven knots tied at equal distances along the length of the wick. (See Figure 13.)

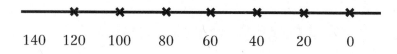

140   120   100   80   60   40   20   0

Figure 13. Knotted wick.

Now make your candle—molded, dipped, jar or whatever, but I'd recommend a jar candle for this—with the 140 end of the wick at the top. When you do your ritual, you will burn the candle in seven stages. You'll light it at the "present" state, where you are smoking 140 cigarettes a week; then let it continue burning until it comes to that first knot. At that point, you will repeat your ritual, getting that added boost from the energy you put into the candle wick when you were preparing it. Ideally, it will take a full day to burn down one knot, so that you repeat your ritual every day with the candle burning continuously. However, if the candle burns down to the next knot before you are ready to start the next day's ritual, extinguish the candle when you can just see the knot starting to surface. You can do your ritual again at the prescribed time, relighting the wick then. By the seventh day, you will be down to the zero point on the wick, and you should have given up smoking. Now allow the candle to burn out completely by itself.

Giving up smoking—or getting rid of any unwanted habit—is hard enough, even Magickally. To have extra power involved can be a big help.

Floating Candles

Another type of candle we'll look at is the floating candle, frequently made in the form of wax flowers. I find it useful, for example, to make pink floating candles to promote love, or light blue or violet ones for meditation.

You can use prepared beeswax sheets, or pour your own sheets from a low-melting-point wax, something containing thirty to fifty percent beeswax. An old cookie-baking pan is good for this. Heat the wax so that it pours out and fills the metal pan to a depth of about one-sixteenth to one-eighth of an inch. To keep the wax supple while you work on it, place the pan on a warming pad, or on a small electric heating pad on a low setting. With a sharp knife, cut out shapes like the petals of a rose. Lift these and work them together, building up a wax flower. You can build up as many layers (petals) as you wish. Keep a short length of wick in the center of the flower as you build it; and again, concentrate on the purpose to which you will be putting this flower candle when it is finished.

Tallow Candles

To make tallow candles the old-fashioned way, cut up chunks of lamb or mutton fat and fry them very slowly in a large kettle over low heat (so as not to burn the fat). Any bits of crackling that appear floating in the resulting hot fat should be skimmed off. When it is all melted, strain it through a cloth, being careful not to burn yourself. Then, in a large kettle, dissolve four pounds of alum in two gallons of water. Add the melted tallow. Stir and simmer for about an hour, skimming off any residue that rises to the top. Slowly cool the mixture until it can be touched, then strain it through a cloth again. Set it aside to harden. When the tallow is hard, you'll find it is floating on top of the water. Lift it off and scrape away the impure layer on the bottom. You now have a large disk of purified tallow ready to use for making candles.

There is a recipe for tallow candles found at the home of President James Monroe in Charlottesville, Virginia. It is as follows:

5 pints tallow

1 pint beeswax (a higher proportion would probably be better)

1 cake camphor (substitute aromatic oil)

1 teaspoon alum (a hardener)

Apparently this is enough to make three to four dozen candles.

Tallow candles are not recommended for candle-burning Magick. They are generally obnoxiously smelly and seldom harden properly.

Additives

Oil-based scent or perfume can be added to candle wax so that the candle will give off a particular smell as it burns. It's best to add the scent just before you actually pour the mold or start the dipping. A quarter of an ounce of pure, undiluted oil is enough to perfume three pounds of wax, so use it sparingly. Another way to add perfume is simply to soak the wick in the oil before making the candle.

Powdered herbs can also be added, and these can be used for their Magickal qualities. They are especially easy to add to beeswax rolled candles by sprinkling in as you roll. (For a list of the properties of some of the more common herbs, see Table 7, "Magickal Properties of Herbs," in the Appendix.)

As mentioned, you can also cut up photographs, or add hair or nail clippings to personalize candles. Do anything you can to make your candles more potent. One nice touch is to drop small coins—dimes or, perhaps even better, the tiny metal coins obtainable at novelty stores—into money candles. As they burn down during a money ritual, you will have the thrill of seeing money suddenly materializing out of the candle itself! It's a little theatrical, but it can be a wonderful psychological boost in the middle of an intense ritual. You can also cut a dollar bill into tiny pieces and incorporate that. You could do the same thing with tiny hearts and other appropriate shapes found at novelty and specialty stores (often tiny sequin hearts are mixed in with confetti at marriage supply stores). In the rituals given in Part Three of this book, you'll find some other suggestions. Be inventive. Be creative. That's what Magick is all about.

VIII

MENTAL PREPARATION

I n Chapter Three I stated that one of the most important ingredients for working Magick is will power. It
follows, then, that the most important preparation
for Magick is mental preparation. You must train yourself to focus exclusively on the object of your desire—
your reason for working the Magick. You will need this
concentration even before the ritual itself, for you will
need it when making the candles and everything else
connected with the ritual.

It's not easy to focus on one thing, or even one subject,
to the exclusion of everything else. It can help to do a few
exercises to achieve this focus. Here are three you might
work with. You'll probably think of others yourself.

Exercise One

Prepare by sitting comfortably and breathing deeply for a few moments. Go through the process of breathing in the white light of purity and protection, and breathing out the blackness and negativity. I cannot stress enough how this needs to be done before every occult ritual. Look upon it as your life preserver; you should never go out in a boat without wearing a life vest, and you should never embark upon any metaphysical exercise without creating your light of protection.

Find a large, color photograph in a magazine. It can be of a house or a scenic picture of a farm or just about anything. (For the moment don't use any portraits of people.) Sit and study the picture, seeing all the details. Let's suppose you are looking at a farm scene with a large oak tree in the left foreground, an old red barn set back in the center, and some cows grazing by a stream off in the distance on the right. Look at the picture. See the shapes and colors, the sunlight and shadows.

Now tear the picture in half down the middle and put the right half away for the moment. Lay the left half on a sheet of white paper and look at it. Look hard and see the missing half of the picture materialize. (Tip: it helps to squint your eyes a little as you do this.) See all the details of that missing half to the point where you could almost swear the picture was whole again. See the whole barn, and see those cows over by the stream. Then reverse the process: put the missing right half back, verify your vision of it, and remove the left half. Again visualize the whole barn and the big tree in the foreground.

The last step, of course, is to remove both halves and still see the complete picture in all its detail.

Exercise Two

Now sit at a table and place a bowl of fruit or flowers in the center of the table. Having settled in your chair and done your light-building, look at the bowl of fruit; but don't *just* look at it—study it. See the arrangement of the fruit. Is the apple against the orange and separated from the pear? Is the banana resting across both apple and orange or orange and pear? Where do the grapes fit in? See and study the whole arrangement of the fruit or flowers in the bowl, and notice the colors and the variations in color within each separate fruit. Note how the shadows fall, and how the different colors contrast. Study it in every detail, until you can close your eyes and still see it perfectly.

This is, in fact, what you are aiming for: to be able to close your eyes and still see every detail. Keep your eyes closed and picture the bowl and its contents. For the first few attempts you will probably need to flick open your eyes a couple of times to verify one aspect or another; but you'll soon get to where you can keep your eyes closed and still see every detail.

When you are able to do this, keep your eyes closed and imagine that the bowl is turning ninety degrees to the left. In your mind see the bowl turning, and note the arrangement of the fruit from the new angle. Again, see the relationships of the various items, and the changes in the shadow patterns. When you feel you have a good picture, open your eyes and gently turn the bowl to see if you were correct. Keep that mental image in your mind and compare the two. Correct your mental image where it's wrong. Turn the bowl back to its original position and repeat the experiment. See if you now have the correct picture. Then go on to turn the bowl another ninety degrees, so that it is now as though you were looking at it from the opposite side of the table. Again study it and see every possible detail, and once again open your eyes and physically turn the bowl to see how accurate you were.

Keep at this exercise until you can mentally turn the bowl of fruit to any angle and still see each and every detail and relationship.

Exercise Three

Take a photograph of someone—a head shot is better than a full-figure picture, though either will suffice. After your light-building preparation, study the picture until you can see the face in your mind's eye, even with your eyes closed. As with Exercise Two, be able to see the face, and then be able to have the head turn to any angle and still see every possible detail.

You may want to have a friend sit for you while you study his or her face rather than a photograph. You can have him or her turn his or her head when you need to verify what you have seen. It's amazing how often you will see a birthmark or something else which you didn't know was there! You will see it in your mind when you mentally turn your friend's head, and it will be confirmed when he or she actually turns his or her head. When you reach this stage, you know you are well prepared for working your Magick.

You will see the importance of the above exercises when you do a Magickal ritual. Let's say that you are working to bring some desperately needed money to a neighbor of yours who has asked you to work for her because she needs to pay off her mortgage before the bank forecloses. (It would still be better if she did it herself but, for the sake of the example, we'll have you do the Magick!)

In order to put sufficient feeling into the ritual, and to focus on the neighbor, you need to be able to see her clearly in your mind. You need to be able to see her as she worries about the lack of money, and you especially need to be able to see her when she is overjoyed at the sudden income that meets her need. In fact, this last visualization is where you will concentrate.

You need to be able to concentrate on the *situation*, going from specifics—people, places, and things—to abstracts—love, health, and satisfaction. This can take more time to develop, but most people get the knack of it fairly easily. It's a matter of developing your natural inner feelings together with your empathy for others.

Ready, Aim, Fire!

In *Buckland's Complete Book of Witchcraft*, I talk about what I term the "Ready, Aim, Fire!" steps to Magick; drawing the analogy of a child pumping up his airgun, aiming it, and squeezing the trigger. The pumping up is the imagining, building up power to be released. (As we proceed you'll see that this step is far more important in advanced candle Magick than it was in basic candle-burning rituals.) "Aiming" is getting a clear picture in your mind of what you want to achieve and directing the energy there. "Firing" is, of course, the actual release of the built-up energy.

Aiming

One of the secrets to successful Magick is to see the finished product—to concentrate on the end result rather than on the steps to getting there. In the above example, rather than seeing your neighbor gradually getting money, and gradually getting out of debt, you would put all your energies into seeing her completely free of debt, happily celebrating her final payment on the mortgage, and receiving the deed to her home. *You would concentrate on the situation as it will be when the Magick has done its work.* If you were working on helping someone recover from a broken leg, you would see them running around and jumping up and down for joy at their recovery. If you were helping someone get over a case of laryngitis, you would see them shouting and singing at the top of their voice. If you were working to bring love to yourself, you would see yourself happily locked in the arms of your lover, not even thinking about the many steps to get to that position.

Building Power in the Ritual

Throughout this book I've been talking about building up power for your Magick. Let's look now at the specifics of that power-building as it will be done in the ritual itself.

In ordinary candleburning rituals, you are using your need for success in the rite to help you put energy into the lighting of the candles and their manipulation. In advanced candle Magick, you should do more than that: you should work up that need and build your power, so that there is a force to be released like a heat-seeking missile, homing in on the ultimate goal you have planned.

In Witchcraft and Voudoun rituals, much of the power-raising for Magick is achieved by dancing and chanting. In ceremonial Magick, there is frequently chanting, though seldom dancing. Other Magickal ritual workers around the globe use variations on these ideas. You don't need to be a Witch to work Magick, but that's not to say that you can't use some of these techniques which have been so effective for so many millennia.

The common denominators in the above examples of Magick-working are beat and rhythm. Dancing and chanting are done to a steady, solid beat, and to a particular rhythm. That rhythm may vary depending upon the object of the exercise, but rhythm of some sort is always present. Listen to your heartbeat. It is a steady, rhythmic beat. Imagine if the beat were amplified tremendously so that you were aware of it pounding in your head. You would move to it; you would dance to that beat; you would sing to that steady rhythm. In fact, many Magicians do just that: they play an amplified recording of a heartbeat and dance and chant to it. Listen to recordings of Voudoun drums, to marching bands, to New Orleans or Chicago-style jazz. The drum beat is the driving force; it propels the music along. This is the effect you want to achieve within your body to get you moving, to get your blood flowing, to build up your psychic energy—your power!

You don't have to lug a drum into your ritual area to achieve this. You can do it all in your head. First you need a Key Word for your ritual. We'll look at various suitable ones in detail later in this book, but for now let's examine the basic ones. All Magick can be divided to fall under one of four main headings: Health, Power, Protection, or Prosperity. (Love would seem to be a fifth possible heading, but it falls under the heading of Power or Prosperity.) You can do all of your Magick with only these four words in your repertoire.

To continue our example, the neighbor lady who needed to pay off her mortgage focuses your ritual on money; so obviously the word for you is going to be "Prosperity." The word "Wealth," as a single syllable, might be easier to concentrate on, so before you light each candle, you will build up the power by chanting the word "Wealth" a number of times. Imagine a steady, single, drum beat. Hear it thumping, and get the rhythm of it. Let your feet tap to it. "Wealth! Wealth! Wealth! Wealth! Wealth!" As you chant, feel the power building up within you. Feel your blood start to pulsate through your body. Feel the energy level climbing. Let it happen—no, *make* it happen—that your whole body is reverberating with that one word: "Wealth!" Then direct that energy into the candle as you light it, or into the tool as you make it, or into the candle as you anoint it. In this way you imbue your Magickal tools with the energy of the ritual. You supercharge them for the Magick to be done.

If you have the room (which you won't have in a closet!), then I do recommend dancing to help the build-up of power. Moving around with your feet stamping the floor, clapping your hands, can really help you approach *ekstasis*, or ecstasy—that Magickal power-producing state of the shamans and medicine-people around the world. Chant and dance together can be formidable.

IX

CANDLE PREPARATION

You have made your candles and imbued them with power in the process. They are specific candles, in that they are either Astral Candles made with a particular person (or type of person) in mind, or they are Offertory Candles made for a special purpose (love, attraction, strength, fertility). Now before you start the actual ritual, these candles must be further prepared by inscribing, if appropriate, to personalize them, and by dressing, or anointing.

Inscriptions

You are going to work for the neighbor lady who needs money to pay off her mortgage. You know her birthdate, so you have the appropriately colored candle, which you made especially hers by mixing in shreds of her photograph and handwriting. This candle is very definitely *her*, yet it can be even more so!

The lady's name is Ethel Brady. The name was one of the things you concentrated on while making the candle, but now you are actually going to engrave the name along its length. To do this you will use your Magickal Awl and one of the Magickal alphabets. (See Table 13, "Magickal Alphabets," in the Appendix.) A Magickal alphabet aids concentration which helps put power into what you write. If you just scratched "Ethel Brady" into the wax, it wouldn't do much in the way of adding to the candle's efficacy; but by using an unusual alphabet—one with which you are not too familiar— you really have to concentrate on what you are doing, on forming each character, which puts energy/power/ manna into the candle.

Let's say you choose to use the Theban alphabet. (See Figure 14.) As you engrave the sigils, you again concentrate on the lady herself. See her; know that this candle represents her, and everything that involves this candle will involve her.

The name should be engraved onto the candle from the wick end to the base. (See Figure 15.) In this way, the

ՂᲜᲧ᠑Ნ᠑ ᎖ᎷᎷᲜᎷᎷᏡ

Figure 14. "Ethel Brady" in Theban.

candle burns down the name in the same direction you would read it, so there is flow; there is no obstruction.

On the other side of the candle, opposite the name side, you can add other engraving if you wish. You could add the lady's astrological signs—Sun, Moon, Ascendant—her birth date, or Birth Number from numerology. You don't have to add this extra information, of course, but every little bit helps. Also, it may be that you don't know the person's name, or their full name. In this case any information you do have should be added.

Figure 15. Theban inscribed candle.

If you are doing a love ritual for an as-yet-unknown lover, then you could use a white candle and inscribe it with the personality traits you want. You could use a candle the color of the astrological sign you would like the person to be, and add other preferred details.

Working on an Offertory Candle is very similar. Let's say you are preparing an orange candle for "Attraction." Inscribe the candle with the word "Attraction," again running down the candle, and written in one of the Magickal alphabets. It is important that, whichever alphabet you choose, you should use that same alphabet for all the candles in that ritual. Do not engrave one candle in Theban, for example, another in Angelic, and another in Runes. Stick to one form of writing for all candles in the particular ritual.

Candle-Anointing Oil

The last thing you do in preparation before the candle is placed on the altar to be lit, is to "dress" it. This is an anointing with oil which is done with the intention of further imbuing the candle with the represented person's attributes or the candle's purpose.

Various oils may be used. If you are dressing a candle for love, you might well use an oil based on rose petals or patchouli. For courage, you would use geranium; and likewise, mint for money. These will be detailed in the rituals which follow. To make a candle-anointing oil, the oil base can be simply olive oil, but use a good quality, virgin olive oil. Take a jar and fill it three-quarters full of the flower or herb you are going to use. Let's take roses as an example. Use only freshly-gathered rose petals, and slowly pour in the oil to cover the petals and fill the jar. Put on the top and let the sealed jar stand for three to four days. Every twenty-four hours, turn the jar upside down.

At the end of that time, take a second jar of equal size and fill it three-quarters full with a new batch of freshly-gathered rose petals. From the first jar, pour the oil into the second jar, straining it through a piece of cheesecloth to hold back the used rose petals, and squeezing it to get out all the oil. Cap the second jar and again let it stand for three to four days, turning it every twenty-four hours. Continue this process of charging the oil with fresh rose petals. After about two weeks you will have an oil that has all the essence of the roses, and is ready to be used to dress candles for love rituals.

Oils for other purposes can be made the same way, steeping the appropriate flower or herb in the oil over a period of time. You can purchase candle-anointing oils, but again, I feel it is far better to make your own.

Dressing the Candle

The candle should be dressed from the center out toward each end. (See Figure 16.) Hold the candle and rub it with oil from the center out to the end; then from the center out to the other end. All the time you are anointing the candle, concentrate on the person the candle represents or the purpose of the candle.

If a candle is used in a ritual, it *must* be anointed. If it is the same candle that is being used in a repeat of a ritual (a ritual that must be done on three Fridays in a row, for example), it must still be anointed for that second or third time, even though it was anointed in a previous rite.

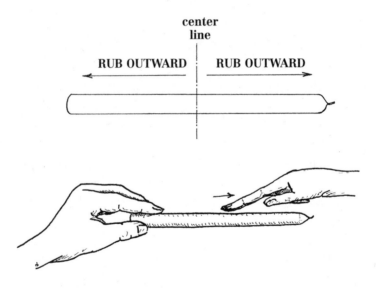

Figure 16. Anointing a candle.

Lighting and Extinguishing Candles

It is best not to light candles directly from a match. It is much better to first light a taper, and then light the candle from the taper.

There has been a lot of nonsense written about extinguishing candles. I've seen it said that you must not blow out a candle. The reason given is that it is an "insult" to the Element of Fire! If you do rituals out in the open air, you will frequently find that the wind will blow out a candle, so I certainly see nothing wrong with it. It can be no insult if there is no *intent*. Having said that, I do think it's better to snuff out a candle, pinching it between the thumb and forefinger. Scott Cunningham described this as "locking in the energy." I think that's a good way of viewing it. Another alternative is to use a candle snuffer.

Now you are ready to start your ritual.

X

PLANNING THE RITUAL

You know what ritual you are going to do. You have made all the candles you will need, together with any poppets or ancillary items. Now it's time to plan the ritual itself.

Timing is one of the most important aspects. You've planned the time of year, phase of the moon, day of the week, and hour of the day or night in which to work. Now look at the ritual, read it through carefully (several times), and decide how long it will take to perform. Almost certainly it will not take more than an hour, but just in case, begin your ritual as close as possible to the start of the hour. (See Chapter Four.) That way all of the ritual will fall within that special hour. When gauging the time needed to do the ritual, don't forget to include the time you will need for building your psychic defenses: breathing in the light and enclosing yourself in the ball of protection.

Don't skimp on the building of power that I talked about in Chapter Eight. Decide exactly *how* you are going to build that power. Are you going to dance about the circle and chant? If so, just how are you going to dance? Have you thought about the actual steps? It's one thing to be extemporaneous, but its something else to find yourself so concerned with the movement of your feet that you are distracted from concentrating on the object of the Magick. Ideally, you should be able to move rhythmically and forcefully to build up your power, yet be able to concentrate on directing that power into the object of the exercise. Perhaps the best thing is simply to stamp rhythmically in time to a steady beat while chanting your Key Word.

Decide on that Key Word ahead of time, too. In the rituals included in this book, a Key Word is suggested, but you may prefer a different one. If you have written your own ritual, you will need to decide on one for that. A rule of thumb is to make it as short as possible; however, a whole phrase can be used if that's what seems most appropriate. For one person, chanting the word "Money" over and over again will work beautifully; to another, the repeated phrase "cash come to me" might be much more effective. On the whole, I'd suggest that the shorter and sharper the chant, the more easily it can be incorporated into the ritual without any great need for thought. You should be chanting it automatically while concentrating your focus on the end result of the Magick you're working.

Know what it is you're going to see as the end result. Know *exactly* what you are "aiming" at. If it's to have money come, then see that money there. If it's for promotion or a new job, then see yourself actually in that position, working happily and successfully. If it's to lose weight, then see yourself slim and trim. Remember, you have to see and concentrate on the successful outcome.

If you will be using photographs or poppets, or anything in addition to the candles, decide beforehand exactly where on your altar set-up they will lie. Know where your matches are, and have the incense and charcoal ready.

PART THREE

THE RITUALS

XI

INTRODUCTION TO
THE RITUALS

I have tried not to duplicate the rituals that appear in *Practical Candleburning Rituals*, and I hope these new ones will supplement those. The rituals in this book may be simplified and performed in the manner of the old, Low Magick, ones; and, conversely, any of the rites in *Practical Candleburning Rituals* may be done in this advanced candle Magick manner.

Over the years I have received many letters from practitioners. I have referred to these letters to see where there is the greatest need for new rituals. In keeping with the unhappy increase in such problem areas as child, spouse, and sexual abuse, I have included rituals addressing these issues.

Don't hesitate to modify the rituals for your comfort. Because they are written for optimum results, do remember that if you take shortcuts, you may affect your chances of success.

Always remember to do your protective light-building before you take your ritual bath.

Where rituals are to be done over a number of days, or even weeks, if at all possible *leave the altar set up from the end of one ritual until the start of the next.* If you *must* dismantle the altar set-up, carefully note the placement of each item, so you can reposition each *exactly* for the next ritual. Where rituals are repeated over several days or weeks, you should also repeat, on the succeeding days, the inscribing and anointing of candles. Simply go over the existing inscription with the Awl.

After doing some of these rituals (and certainly reading all of them), do write your own rituals, incorporating all that I have presented in this book. Study the rituals that follow to see why and how they were constructed. For your own rituals, determine the purpose, the person or people involved, and the candles and their relevant colors. Decide whether you should make special candles in the sense of incorporating additives (See Chapter Eight), and what, if any, supplementary items are called for. Would an image candle be better for the Petitioner, or for other Astral Candles? Would a seven-knob candle be appropriate for a ritual to be done over a one-week period? When would a photograph help, and should you use a placket? Determine your Key Word so that you can really put power into what you do. Don't forget to settle on just the right incense, oil, and bath salts; and most importantly, take the time to work out the best possible hours and the most effective days.

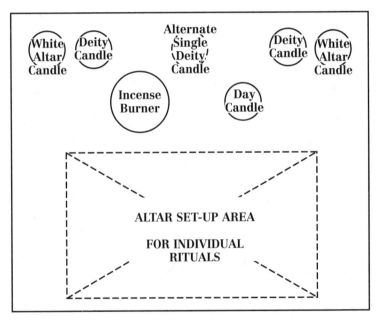

Figure 17. Suggested basic altar layout.
(Modify if necessary to suit your own requirements.)

TO ACCEPT A SITUATION

It is frequently difficult for us to accept a situation that has been forced upon us. Separation, divorce, loss of a job, illnesses such as cancer or AIDS; none of these is easy to deal with, and many people suffer tremendous mental anguish in trying to adjust. This ritual can be very effective in bringing you to acceptance of a situation.

Timing
To be started in the waning cycle of the Moon, and done over a period of three consecutive days each week for three weeks (a total of nine times)

Day(s)
Friday, Saturday, Sunday

Hour
Mercury

Candles
Astral for Petitioner (the one requesting help); Day candles as appropriate; Offertory: Dark Blue (3) inscribed "Understanding," Light Blue (6) inscribed "Acceptance," White (9) inscribed "Peace"

Incense
Rosemary or sandalwood

Oil
Equal parts carnation, rosemary, and sandalwood

Key Word
"Blend"

Supplementary Items
Photograph of Petitioner; Placket (green and light blue)

Bath
Equal parts rose geranium, rosemary, and violet

Breathe deeply and build your ball of protective light. While soaking in your ritual bath, meditate on the whole ritual, the steps you will take, and the end you have in mind. Enter the Circle in the hour of Mercury on the first Friday and stand, kneel, or sit before the altar. Light the incense. With the Oil, dress the Altar

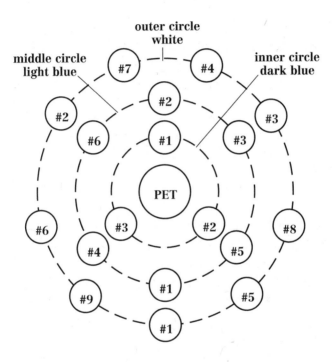

Altar Set-up #1
"To Accept a Situation"

Candles and the Day Candle, while concentrating on the
purpose of the ritual.

Light your taper; then, from that, light the Altar
Candles and the Day Candle. State your intent:

> *I am here to help [Name] accept [his/her] situation;
> to blend in once again with those around and to look
> forward with pleasure to the positive aspects of life.*

or

> *I am here to help myself, [Name], to accept my situ-
> ation; to blend in once again with those around me
> and to look forward with pleasure to the positive
> aspects of life.*

With the Awl, inscribe the Petitioner's name on the
Astral Candle, then dress the candle with Oil, remembering to concentrate on the Petitioner while doing so.

Take up the photograph and study it for a few
moments, reviewing all that you know of the Petitioner,
and joining your love and strength with his/hers. If
others have sent their love to join with you and the
Petitioner, see it all coming together, surrounding the
figure in the photograph. Hold the photograph in the
smoke of the incense for a moment, concentrating on
the Key Word "Blend," then slip the photograph inside
the Placket and place it under the Petitioner Candle in
the center of the altar.

With your taper, light the Petitioner Candle and say:

This is [Name], who has the strength to overcome all
negativity. Let [his/her] spirit burn as surely as does
this flame; a symbol of the inner strength that will
prevail in all things.

With the Awl, inscribe all three of the Dark Blue
Candles each with the word "Understanding." Dress
them with Oil.
Light the Dark Blue #1 Candle and say:

Here do I light the first lamp of Understanding. May
its light ease the burden placed on shoulders not yet
strong.

Take up the Censer and swing it, censing the whole
area around the altar, while rhythmically repeating
the Key Word "Blend," and building up the energy to
that focus. Replace the Censer and direct your energies
toward the Petitioner Candle. Say:

The winds blow across the sands
Raising the dunes in irregular shapes.
Small and large; wide and narrow.
There seems no rhyme nor reason
To these barriers erected
On the seashore.
Why should this happen?
Why here and not elsewhere?
Why cannot the sands be soft and smooth forever?

But in the fullness of time the waves come.
They sweep across and gently chide the dunes.
They slip in between;
They roll up and over and across.
Slowly, imperceptibly,
The dunes smooth down.
Slowly, imperceptibly,
The dunes blend into the sands around them.
Slowly, imperceptibly,
All becomes one.

See in your mind the Petitioner happy and laughing, at peace with his/her situation; accepting it and concentrating on the positive aspects of life. Concentrate your thoughts on this end object: the Petitioner happy, accepting, and blending in with his/her friends and surroundings. You may remain there with these thoughts for as long as you wish. Then extinguish the candles in reverse order to that in which they were lit. Leave the altar set up.

The following day (Saturday), at the appropriate time (hour of Mercury), again enter the circle after your ritual bath, and again light the Altar Candles. Dress the new Day candle, light it, and then state your intent:

I am here to help [Name] accept [his/her] situation;
to blend in once again with those around and to look
forward with pleasure to the positive aspects of life.

Inscribe, anoint, and light the Petitioner Candle and say:

This is [Name], who has the strength to overcome all negativity. Let [his/her] spirit burn as surely as does this flame; a symbol of the inner strength that will prevail in all things.

Inscribe, anoint, and light the Dark Blue #1 and #2 Candles and say:

Here do I light the first and the second lamps of Understanding. May their light ease the burden placed on shoulders not yet strong.

Take up the Censer and swing it, censing the whole area around the altar while chanting the Key Word. Build up the energy to that focus. Replace the Censer and direct your energies toward the Petitioner Candle. Say:

The winds blow across the sands
Raising the dunes in irregular shapes.
Small and large; wide and narrow.
There seems no rhyme nor reason
To these barriers erected
On the seashore.
Why should this happen?
Why here and not elsewhere?
Why cannot the sands be soft and smooth forever?
But in the fullness of time the waves come.
They sweep across and gently chide the dunes.

They slip in between;
They roll up and over and across.
Slowly, imperceptibly,
The dunes smooth down.
Slowly, imperceptibly,
The dunes blend into the sands around them.
Slowly, imperceptibly,
All becomes one.

Again concentrate your thoughts on the end object. See in your mind the Petitioner happy and laughing, at peace with his/her situation; accepting it and concentrating on the positive aspects of life. You may remain with these thoughts for as long as you wish. Then extinguish the candles in reverse order to that in which they were lit. Leave the altar set up.

The following day (Sunday), at the hour of Jupiter, again enter the circle after your ritual bath, and again light the Altar Candles, dress the new Day candle, light it, and state your intent:

I am here to help [Name] accept [his/her] situation;
to blend in once again with those around and to look
forward with pleasure to the positive aspects of life.

Inscribe, anoint, and light the Petitioner Candle and say:

This is [Name], who has the strength to overcome all
negativity. Let [his/her] spirit burn as surely as does

this flame, a symbol of the inner strength that will prevail in all things.

Inscribe, anoint, and light the Dark Blue #1, #2, and #3 Candles and say:

Here do I light the first, second, and third lamps of Understanding. May their light ease the burden placed on shoulders not yet strong.

Take up the Censer and swing it, censing the whole area around the altar. Again chant the Key Word and build up the energy to that focus. Replace the Censer and direct your energies toward the Petitioner Candle. Say:

The winds blow across the sands
Raising the dunes in irregular shapes.
Small and large; wide and narrow.
There seems no rhyme nor reason
To these barriers erected
On the seashore.
Why should this happen?
Why here and not elsewhere?
Why cannot the sands be soft and smooth forever?
But in the fullness of time the waves come.
They sweep across and gently chide the dunes.
They slip in between;
They roll up and over and across.
Slowly, imperceptibly,
The dunes smooth down.
Slowly, imperceptibly,

The dunes blend into the sands around them.
Slowly, imperceptibly,
All becomes one.

Again concentrate your thoughts on the end object. See in your mind the Petitioner happy and laughing, at peace with his/her situation; accepting it and concentrating on the positive aspects of life. You may remain with these thoughts for as long as you wish. Then extinguish the candles in reverse order to that in which they were lit. Leave the altar set up.

The following week, starting on Friday, repeat the above ritual, but this time, immediately after you have lit the three Dark Blue Candles and stated their purpose, you will take the six Light Blue Candles and inscribe each of them with the word "Acceptance." Then you will dress them with Oil. Now light the Light Blue #1 and #2 Candles, saying:

Here do I light the first lamps of Acceptance. May their light strengthen the shoulders that had been worn down.

Continue as above, with the censing, chanting, the poem, and concentration.

The following day (Saturday) repeat the ritual, lighting all the Dark Blue Candles with the words:

Here do I light the lamps of Understanding. May their light ease the burden placed on shoulders not yet strong.

Then light the Light Blue Candles #1, #2, #3, and #4, saying:

Here do I light the lamps of Acceptance. May their light strengthen the shoulders that had been worn down.

Continue with the censing, chanting, poem, and concentration, as before.

The following day (Sunday) you will light all the Dark Blue Candles with the appropriate words, and all the Light Blue Candles with their appropriate words, followed again by the censing, chanting, the poem, and concentration, before extinguishing the candles and leaving them set up.

The third week you will repeat the process, but this time you will inscribe the White Candles with the word "Peace," and anoint them. Then you will repeat the ritual adding the first three White Candles (#1, #2, and #3) on Friday, the first six on Saturday and, on Sunday, lighting all candles in order. For these White Candles you will say:

Here do I light the lamps of Peace. May [Name] find that peace in [his/her] life from now on, accepting what cannot be changed and enjoying all that is positive and good.

You will continue each time with the censing, chanting, poem, and concentration before extinguishing all candles.

At the end of the final Sunday ritual, you will leave the candles to burn down for at least twenty-four hours. At the end of that time you may either leave them to burn out altogether, or you may extinguish them.

TO BE NOTICED
BY ONE YOU ADMIRE

You may be attracted to someone, but they don't seem to know that you exist. You feel sure that if only they would notice you there might be a chance to start a relationship. Here is a ritual that will help you be noticed by one you admire.

Timing
To be started in the waxing cycle of the Moon, and repeated every Thursday throughout that cycle, and for the following two waxing cycles (over a three-month period in all)

Day(s)
Thursday

Hour
Mars

Candles
Astral for Petitioner; Day: Blue; Offertory: White (4) inscribed with name if known, leave blank if no one in particular; Orange/Yellow (4) inscribed "Attraction" and "Encouragement"

Incense
Equal parts basil and cinnamon, or benzoin, pepperwort, and wood aloes

Oil
Lavender and mint for dressing White Candles. Ambergris, cinnamon, musk, and patchouli for male Petitioner, and four Orange/Yellow Candles; ambergris, jasmine, and violet for female Petitioner, and four Orange/Yellow candles

Key Word
"Overt" or "Observe"

Supplementary Items
Quartz crystal

Bath
Jasmine, lavender, and rose

Breathe deeply and build your ball of protective light. While soaking in your ritual bath, meditate on the

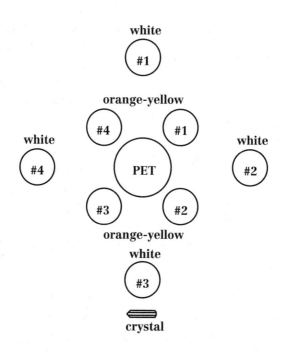

Altar Set-up #2
"To be Noticed"

whole ritual. See yourself as someone who is very attractive, and who would definitely be noticed if only you could catch the eye. Enter the Circle in the hour of Mars on Thursday, and stand, sit, or kneel before the altar. Light the incense. Dress the Altar Candles and the Day Candle with Oil. Light your taper, then light the Altar Candles and the Day Candle. State your intent:

> *I am here to help [Petitioner's Name], a person who is naturally attractive. Such is the attraction of this person that [he/she] will be seen and observed by those desired.*

Take the Awl and inscribe the Petitioner Candle with the name, then dress it with Oil while thinking of the Petitioner. Light the Petitioner Candle and say:

> *This is [Name], a wonderful, attractive person whose company is sought by many.*

Inscribe the four White Candles with the name of the one whose attention you wish to catch, if known. Otherwise, leave them blank. Anoint them with Oil. Light White Candles #1, #2, #3, and #4. Say:

> *All about [Petitioner's Name] are those who would benefit from knowing [him/her].*

With the Awl, inscribe the four Orange/Yellow Candles with the word "Attraction" or "Desire," and anoint them with Oil. Light Orange/Yellow Candle #1 and say:

Here is the attraction, the desirability, of [Petitioner's Name], surrounding [him/her] and reaching out to all.

Take the Crystal in your right hand (or left, if left-handed), and move it from Orange/Yellow #1 to White #1, around that candle and back to Orange/Yellow #1 (see diagram). Then move it from Orange/Yellow #1 around White #2 and back; and similarly around White #3 and then White #4. As you do this, chant the Key Word, "Observe" (or "Overt"), and see your attraction radiating out to everyone around you. If there is someone in particular, see that person looking at you and smiling.

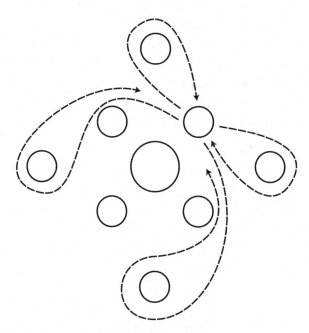

Movement of the crystal.

Light Orange/Yellow Candle #2, and repeat the above, this time moving the Crystal from Orange/Yellow #2 around White #1, #2, #3, and then #4, with the same words and chant.

Repeat for Orange/Yellow Candle #3, and then again for Orange/Yellow Candle #4.

Replace the Crystal on the altar. Sit for a few moments seeing the one desired (or any number of people) smiling and moving across to speak with you/ Petitioner. After a while, extinguish the candles in the opposite order to that in which they were lit.

Repeat the ritual the next Thursday, and a third Thursday only if it falls within the waxing phase of the Moon. Then wait for the waxing phase of the next month, and repeat the ritual on the Thursdays. (Remember that even though all the candles have now been inscribed and dressed, you must still repeat that process in the follow-up rituals.) The following month repeat on the appropriate Thursdays.

TO BRING ABOUT A RECONSIDERATION

A decision has been made that affects you. It could be a job situation, love or marriage, or any other situation. If you are not happy with the decision and wish that the person(s) responsible would reconsider, then do this ritual.

Timing
Daily for three days, break for three days, daily for three more days, break for three days, daily for three final days (nine days in all)

Day(s)
Start on a Saturday

Hour
Moon

Candles
Astral for Petitioner; Day Candles as appropriate; Offertory: Dark Blue (1) inscribed "Changeability," Light Blue (1) inscribed "Understanding/Patience," Gray (or Silver) (1) inscribed "Neutral"

Incense
Thyme, or equal parts birch bark, dragon's blood, and juniper

Oil
Apple blossom, patchouli, and rose, or three ounces of olive oil, with one drop each of clove and patchouli

Key Word
"Review"

Supplementary Items
Wand

Bath
Frankincense, rose geranium, and rosemary

Breathe deeply and build your ball of protective light. While soaking in your ritual bath, meditate on the whole ritual. How would you like the decision that was made to be reconsidered? Enter the Circle in the hour of the Moon on a Saturday, and stand, kneel, or sit before the altar. Light the incense. With the Oil, dress the Altar Candles and the Day Candle, while concentrating on the

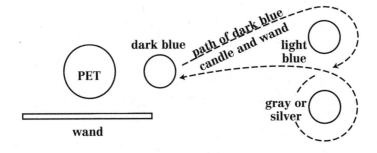

dark blue

PET

wand

path of dark blue candle and wand

light blue

gray or silver

Altar Set-up #3
"To Bring About a Reconsideration"

purpose of the ritual. Light the taper, then light the Altar and Day Candles and state your intent:

I am here to bring about a review of the situation and to have the decision reconsidered.

With the Awl, inscribe the Petitioner's name on the Astral Candle, and then dress the candle with Oil. With your taper, light the Petitioner Candle and say:

This is [Name], who has the strength to accept any final decision made. Let [his/her] spirit burn as surely as does this flame; a symbol of the inner strength that will prevail no matter what the final outcome.

Take the Dark Blue Candle and, with the Awl, inscribe the word "Changeability" on it. Then dress it with Oil, light it, and say:

Here stands the decision made. But it is not irreversible. There is always room for change.

Inscribe the Light Blue Candle with the word "Understanding" on one side, and "Patience" on the other. Dress it with Oil, light it, and say:

Here is patience and understanding for the one who makes the final decision. May [he/she] aid in bringing about a truly dispassionate verdict.

Inscribe the Silver Candle with the word "Neutral," dress it, light it, and say:

Here stands neutrality, ensuring that the final decision is fair.

Swing the incense around the area while chanting the Key Word "Review." If you wish, put down the Censer and continue chanting as you dance about the area. When you feel you have worked up sufficient energy, take up the Dark Blue Candle and move it across the altar, around first the Light Blue, and then the Silver Candle, and back to its place (see diagram). Keep chanting the whole time. Then take up the Wand and touch its tip to the Dark Blue Candle. Pointing with the Wand's tip, trace the same route around the candles three times, chanting louder and louder, and more and more intensely, finishing with a *shout* of the word "Review!"

Replace the Wand, sit quietly, and see the situation with the new decision as you would wish it to be. After some moments of this, extinguish the candles in reverse order to the way they were lit.

The next day, Sunday, repeat the ritual starting in the hour of Mercury, and remembering to change and dress the Day Candle. Do it one more time the following day, Monday, again changing the Day Candle. Repeat the cycle the following Friday, Saturday, and Sunday, then a third set the next Thursday, Friday, and Saturday. You finish on the same day of the week that you started—a Saturday.

TO COMMUNICATE WITH SPIRIT

When someone close to you dies, you often wish, too late, that you had had a chance to say or tell them something before they departed. There are also times when you wish you could communicate with someone who, perhaps, has been dead for some time. With this ritual, the bridging of that gulf is easier. My book, *Doors to Other Worlds* (Llewellyn Publications, 1993) covers spirit communication in detail, but here is a ritual you can use to communicate with candle Magick.

Timing
This ritual can be done at any time, although ideal times are the night of the Full Moon and the night of the New Moon

Hour
Jupiter or Mercury

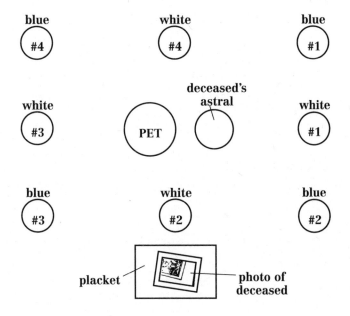

Altar Set-up #4
"To Communicate with Spirit"

Candles
Astral (2): Petitioner and Spirit Contact; Day Candle as appropriate; Offertory: White (4) inscribed "Truth," Blue (4) inscribed "Peace"

Incense
Cinnamon and frankincense or sandalwood

Oil
Equal parts jasmine, lemon, rose, and sandalwood

Key Word
"Communicate"

Supplementary Items
Photograph of deceased; Placket (light blue and violet)

Bath
Lavender, mint, and orange bergamot, or almond and anise

Breathe deeply and build your ball of protective light. While soaking in your ritual bath, meditate on the whole ritual: the steps you will take, your feelings toward the deceased, and what you want to discuss. Enter the Circle in the hour of Jupiter or Mercury, and stand, kneel, or sit before the altar. Light the incense. With the Oil, dress the Altar Candles and the Day Candle, while concentrating on the purpose of the ritual.

Light your taper; then from that, light the Altar Candles and the Day Candle. State your intent:

I am here to communicate with [Name]. I desire to blend once again with [him/her], and look forward with pleasure to that exchange.

With the Awl, inscribe the Petitioner's name on the Petitioner's Astral Candle, and then dress the candle with Oil.

With your taper, light the Petitioner Candle and say:

Here stand I, [Name]. My love for [Deceased's Name] is strong and lasting. Such is that strength that it can reach across the boundaries and through the veil between this world and the next.

I am the one who would draw back the veil. Let the light of this candle shine through and draw my friend to me once again. Let us be together for a while so that we might speak, listen, and communicate.

With the Awl, inscribe all four of the White Candles with the word "Truth." Dress them with Oil.

Light the White #1, #2, #3, and #4 candles and say:

Here do I light the flames of Truth. May this light bring the truth through the veil of the worlds, allowing [Deceased's Name] to come to me again.

Light the Light Blue #1, #2, #3, and #4 candles and say:

Here burn the flames of Peace. Let there be peace between our worlds, that the comings and goings of the spirits may be eased.

Take up the Censer and swing it, censing the whole area around the altar, while rhythmically repeating the Key Word "Communicate," and building up the energy to that focus. Replace the Censer.

Hold the photograph of the deceased in both hands and study it for a few moments, reviewing all that you know of him/her. Hold the photograph in the smoke of the incense, then lay it on the altar. Take up the Deceased's Astral candle, and carve his/her name on it, then anoint it with Oil. Light it and say:

> *I call [Deceased's Name] to me. Let [his/her] spirit return here for a brief time, that I may once again communicate with [him/her].*

Place the Placket, with photograph enclosed, under the Deceased's Astral candle.

Now sit quietly and wait. Focus your attention on the flame of the Deceased's Candle. You will slowly become aware of a figure standing in your peripheral vision. Do not try to look directly at this figure; keep your eyes on the candle. Know that he/she is there and you may start your conversation.

Eventually the figure will fade away. Continue sitting quietly for a few moments, then extinguish the candles in reverse order to the way they were lighted.

TO END AN INCARNATION

This is not a ritual to be used to "terminate" someone you dislike! It is a ritual to be used when someone who is terminally ill, and perhaps in constant pain, has requested you to help ease them through the final doorway. It will do just that—help them pass into the light, shedding the pain and suffering they are experiencing as their present physical incarnation draws to a close.

Timing
To be started in the waning cycle of the Moon and done over a period of three consecutive days each week for three weeks (a total of nine times)

Day(s)
Friday, Saturday, Sunday

Hour
Moon or Mercury

Candles
Astral for Petitioner (the one requesting help); Day candles as appropriate; Offertory: Dark Blue (3) inscribed "Endings," Light Blue (3) inscribed "Rebirth," White (3) inscribed "Beginnings"

Incense
Cinnamon, frankincense, myrrh, rose petals, and vervain

Oil
Equal parts gardenia, jasmine, and lotus

Key Word
"Transformation"

Supplementary Items
Photograph of Petitioner; Placket (light and dark blue)

Bath
Eucalyptus, gardenia, lotus, and sandalwood

Breathe deeply and build your ball of protective light. While soaking in your ritual bath, meditate on the whole ritual: the steps you will take and the Petitioner's gentle transition into the light. Enter the Circle in the hour of the Moon or Mercury on the first Friday and stand, kneel, or sit before the altar. Light the incense.

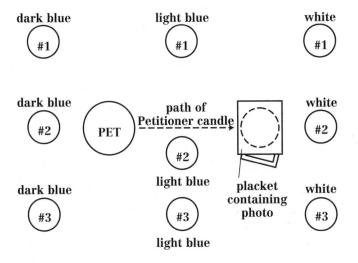

Altar Set-up #5
"To End an Incarnation"

With the Oil, dress the Altar Candles and the Day Candle, while concentrating on the purpose of the ritual.

Light your taper; then from that, light the Altar Candles and the Day Candle. State your intent:

> *I am here to help [Name] accept [his/her] situation and to pass on through the portals that separate this world from the next. I am here to help make the transition easier through an abundance of light and love.*

With the Awl, inscribe the Petitioner's name on the Astral Candle, then dress the candle with Oil.

Take up the photograph and study it for a few moments, reviewing all that you know of the Petitioner, and joining your love and strength with his/hers. If others have sent their love to join with you and the Petitioner, then see it all coming together, surrounding the figure in the photograph. Hold the photograph in the smoke of the incense for a moment, concentrating on the Key Word "Transformation," then slip the photograph inside the Placket and place it alongside and to the left of the White #2 Candle (see altar set-up).

With your taper, light the Petitioner Candle and say:

> *This is [Name], who has the strength to overcome all negativity. Let [his/her] spirit burn as surely as does this flame; a symbol of the inner strength that will prevail in all things, carrying [him/her] through to the light.*

With the Awl, inscribe all three of the Dark Blue Candles with the word "Endings." Dress them with Oil.
Light the Dark Blue Candles #1, #2, and #3 and say:

Here do I light the first flames of Understanding, shedding light onto the past and opening the way to the future. Let the life that was lived be ended, with joy and happiness in the knowledge that it was lived to the fullest.

With the Awl, inscribe all three of the Light Blue Candles with the word "Rebirth." Dress them with Oil.
Light the Light Blue Candles #1, #2, and #3 and say:

Here burn the flames of Rebirth. With the past behind, only the future can lie ahead. Passing through these flames signals the start of the journey; the move into the light and all that lies beyond.

With the Awl, inscribe all three of the White Candles with the word "Beginnings." Dress them with Oil.
Light the White Candles #1, #2, and #3 and say:

With the light from these candles, the feet are firmly on the path of the new life. Here is the beginning of the adventure that will lead beyond the light into the future.

Take up the Censer and swing it, censing the whole area around the altar, while rhythmically repeating the Key Word "Transformation," and building up the

energy to that focus.   Replace the Censer and direct
your energies toward the Petitioner Candle. Say:

*Through the forces of love may the bonds that hold
the physical body here be broken. Through the forces
of love let the old shell slough off to reveal the beauty
of the inner light. Let that light merge and blend with
the radiance of a thousand suns, becoming one with
God/Goddess/All-That-Is in the world beyond. Here
ends a life on this plane of existence, but here begins
a new life on the next plane.*

Very slowly move the Petitioner's Candle to the right.
Slide it gently across the top of the altar, past the line of
Light Blue Candles, to the White ones. Place it on the
Placket containing the Petitioner's photograph. Sit now
and concentrate on the Petitioner having an easy transition out of this life. Surround the figure with love, and see
him/her slipping gently away, out of the physical body.

After several minutes of this concentration, extinguish the candles in the opposite order to that in which
they were lit.

Repeat the whole ritual—with the Petitioner's Candle back in the starting position—each specified day.
Each time, start the ritual in the hour of either the Moon
or Mercury.

TO FIND HAPPINESS

True happiness can oftentimes be elusive, but it is attainable. This ritual may help you find it.

Timing
To be started in the waxing cycle of the Moon, and done over a period of three consecutive days

Day(s)
Thursday, Friday, Saturday

Hour
Venus

Candles
Astral for Petitioner; Day Candles as appropriate; Offertory: Orange (4) inscribed "Happiness," Red (1) inscribed "Strength"

Incense
Copal, frankincense, myrrh, and sandalwood, or dragon's blood, frankincense, and myrrh, or juniper berries and rosemary

Oil
Gardenia, jasmine, and lotus, or patchouli, rose, sandalwood, and vanilla

Key Word
"Happiness"

Supplementary Items
Rose quartz crystals (4)

Bath
Carnation, cinnamon, and violet

Breathe deeply and build your ball of protective light. While soaking in your ritual bath, meditate on the whole ritual: the steps you will take that will lead to your state of happiness. Enter the Circle in the hour of Venus on the first Thursday and stand, kneel, or sit before the altar. Light the incense. With the Oil, dress the Altar Candles and the Day Candle, while concentrating on the purpose of the ritual.

Light your taper, then from that, light the Altar Candles and the Day Candle. State your intent:

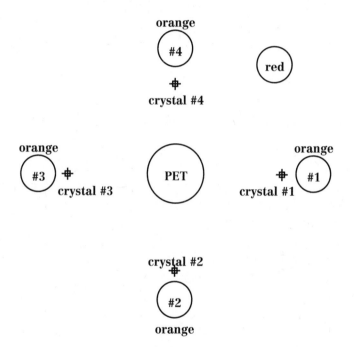

Altar Set-up #6
"To Find Happiness"

I am here to bring happiness to [Name]; to have [him/her] blend with those joyous forces around and about so that [he/she] may look forward with pleasure to all aspects of life.

With the Awl, inscribe the Petitioner's name on the Astral Candle, and then dress the candle with Oil.

With your taper, light the Petitioner's Astral Candle and say:

This is [Name], who has the strength to overcome all negativity. Let [his/her] spirit burn as surely as does this flame; a symbol of the inner strength that will prevail in all things.

With the Awl, inscribe all four of the Orange Candles with the word "Happiness." Dress them with Oil.

Light the Orange #1 Candle and say:

Here do I light the first lamp of Happiness. May its light spread into all corners of the world.

Light the Orange #2 Candle and say:

Here do I light the second lamp of Happiness. May its light join with that of the first to brighten all lives.

Light the Orange #3 Candle and say:

Here do I light the third lamp of Happiness. May it, too, drive out all shadows so that every surface may be bright with the joy of Happiness.

Light the Orange #4 Candle and say:

*Here do I light the fourth lamp of Happiness knowing
that now the circle is complete, and there is no longer
room for darkness and shadow.*

Take up the Censer and swing it, censing the whole
area around the altar, while rhythmically repeating the
Key Word "Happiness," and building up the energy to
that focus. Replace the Censer.

Move the Petitioner's Candle slowly up to touch the
Orange #1 Candle, and then back to its place in the center. Take Crystal #1 and move that down to rest against
the Petitioner's Candle. As you make these moves say:

*Looking outward in all directions, I see the happiness
I seek. It is there, able to be grasped. I will reach out
and seize it! I will draw it in to become a part of me.*

Move the Petitioner's Candle slowly across to touch
the Orange #2 Candle, and then back to its place in
the center. Take Crystal #2 and move that back to rest
against the Petitioner's Candle. As you make these
moves, say:

*Looking outward in all directions, I see the happiness
I seek. It is there, able to be grasped. I will reach out
and seize it! I will draw it in to become a part of me.*

Move the Petitioner's Candle slowly down to touch
the Orange #3 Candle, and then back to its place in the

center. Take Crystal #3 and move that up to rest against the Petitioner's Candle. As you make these moves, say:

Looking outward in all directions, I see the happiness I seek. It is there, able to be grasped. I will reach out and seize it! I draw it in to become a part of me. It is now all around me.

Move the Petitioner's Candle slowly across to touch the Orange #4 Candle, and then back to its place in the center. Take Crystal #4 and move that back to rest against the Petitioner's Candle. As you make these moves, say:

I now have Happiness. It is here; it is all around me. I seize Happiness and make it a part of me. Happiness and I are one!

Take up the Red Candle, inscribe it with the word "Strength," anoint it and light it. Holding it off the surface of the altar, move it around the four Orange Candles in a clockwise direction, while chanting the word "Happiness" over and over again. Move it around the candle group nine times, then set it down alongside the Astral Candle. Three times say:

Here is Strength to keep hold of Happiness. It is mine by rights and will always be a part of me.

Sit for a few minutes knowing that happiness is now a part of your life. Feel happy; enjoy the feeling. When you are ready, extinguish the candles in reverse order.

Repeat the ritual the next day (Friday), and the day after that (Saturday), each time resetting the altar as it was at the start.

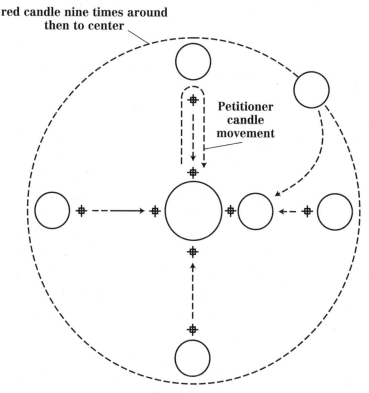

Movements of Petitioner candle and crystals.

TO FIND THE PERFECT MATE

What is "the perfect mate"? Is it someone who laughs when you laugh; who cries when you cry? Someone who is warm, tender, and loving? Someone who respects you as a person and encourages you in your interests? Whatever your definition, the perfect mate seems hard to find for many people. Some are even desperate enough to take any mate they can find, regardless of suitability! This ritual is designed to transmit your energies and use them to attract—in the sense that a magnet attracts metal—someone of the same sensibilities as yourself.

Before you start, you need to be aware of who and what you are. Take the time to sit down, with paper and pencil—yes, write this down—and make a list of your interests, your likes and dislikes, ambitions big and

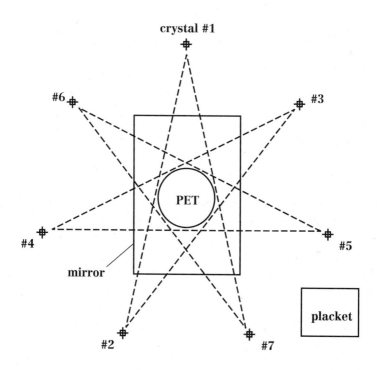

Altar Set-up #7
"To Find the Perfect Mate"

small. Describe yourself as fully as you are able. *Then* you will be better able to judge what you want in another.

Timing
To be done on seven consecutive Fridays, starting in the waxing cycle of the Moon

Day(s)
Friday

Hour
Venus

Candles
Astral for Petitioner, with miniature hearts mixed into the candle (see Chapter Seven, "Additives"); Day: Green

Incense
Benzoin and dragon's blood, or basil, benzoin, and cinnamon

Oil
Olive oil (3 oz.) with a drop of clove and three drops of patchouli

Key Word
"Harmony"

Supplementary Items
Small mirror; Placket (pink and yellow); Seven sacred Stones (agate, amazonite, beryl, jade, opal, rose quartz,

turquoise—these may be small, but the opal should be larger than the others)

Bath
Catnip, elder, lovage, and rose

Breathe deeply and build your ball of protective light. While soaking in your ritual bath, meditate on the whole ritual: the steps you will take and the type of person you have in mind as your ideal mate. Enter the Circle in the hour of Venus on the first Friday (during the waxing Moon), and stand, kneel, or sit before the altar. The seven Stones should be inside the Placket. Light the incense. With the Oil, dress the Altar Candles and the Day Candle, while concentrating on the purpose of the ritual.

Light your taper; then from that, light the Altar Candles and the Day Candle. State your intent:

I, [Petitioner's Name], am here to draw the perfect mate to myself and to blend with [him/her]. I know that I have a lifetime of happiness and pleasure to look forward to.

With the Awl, inscribe the Petitioner's name on the Astral Candle, and then dress the candle with Oil. Stand it on the mirror. *Do not light it.* Say:

This is me, [Name]. I stand here in strength and with the power and discernment to overcome all obstacles and setbacks in my search for the ideal mate. I know

what I seek! I here send out my energies to the uni-
verse, knowing that they will draw back the one who
is right for me, the one who is the ideal mate.

Take up the Placket and hold it between the palms of
your hands. Close your eyes and concentrate your energies into the Placket. Feel all your psychic powers flowing
into the bag and being absorbed by the Stones. Then,
with your right hand (left, if left-handed), hold the Placket
to your heart and, still with your eyes closed, see the
power radiating from the bag and from your heart out
into the universe in all directions. Send it out, with love.

Now take the Stones from the Placket, one at a time,
and lay them on the altar around the Candle in the
order shown. It doesn't matter which order they come
out of the bag, but the first one you draw will be placed
above the candle in the number one position, the second in the number two position, and so on, forming a
seven-pointed star.

Take up the Censer and swing it, censing the whole
area around the altar, while rhythmically repeating the
Key Word "Harmony," and building up the energy, seeing yourself held in an embrace with your ideal.

Replace the Censer and direct your energies toward
the Petitioner Candle. Light it and say:

Here burns the spirit of [Name], who seeks the one
true mate. Let this mirror reflect out all the energies,
all the love and yearning, that I hold in store for the

one I desire. As the days and the weeks pass by let
this energy keep radiating out, constantly impelled
to finally focus on that One and draw [him/her] here.

Now sit, and, with eyes closed, chant again the Key
Word "Harmony." Chant for a few minutes, then be
silent and see, in your mind's eye, yourself with your
true mate. See the two of you together. See the two of
you embracing, loving, sharing, being a part of each
other. Feel the happiness and the joy that permeates the
relationship. *Know that it will be!*

Extinguish the candles in the opposite order they
were lit. Repeat the entire ritual every Friday for the
next six weeks (seven times in all). Your true love will
come to you within three Moons of finishing the ritual.

TO MEET A FINANCIAL OBLIGATION

In this day and age, most people have financial obligations of one sort or another, and it's certainly not unusual for some to find themselves having difficulties meeting their obligations. While it's not possible, Magickally, to bring money just for the sake of having money, it is frequently conceivable that you can "conjure" money that is desperately needed. This ritual is one that is aimed at accomplishing just that.

Timing
To be started in the waxing cycle of the Moon, on a Wednesday, and done over a period of seven consecutive days

Day(s)
Wednesday, Thursday, Friday, Saturday, Sunday, Monday, Tuesday

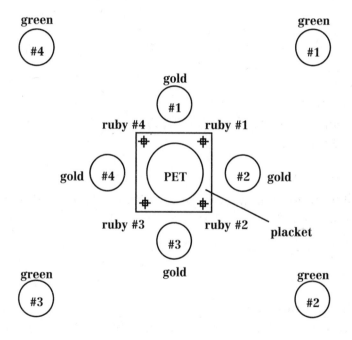

Altar Set-up #8
"To Meet a Financial Obligation"

Hour
Mercury

Candles
Astral for Petitioner; Day Candles as appropriate (may use a seven-day or seven-knob candle if desired); Offertory: Gold (4) two inscribed "Need," and two inscribed "Attraction," Green (4) inscribed "Money" (see Chapter Seven, "Additives")

Incense
Allspice and cedar or cinnamon, clove, lemon balm, and nutmeg

Oil
Cinnamon, mint, patchouli, and pine for Gold Candles; cinnamon, clove, and nutmeg for Green Candles

Key Word
"Money"

Supplementary Items
Rubies (4); Placket (green and light blue)

Bath
Basil, cinnamon, and patchouli

Breathe deeply and build your ball of protective light. While soaking in your ritual bath, meditate on the whole ritual: the steps you will take and the fact that you will get the money to meet your obligations. Enter the Circle in the hour of Mercury and stand, kneel, or sit before the altar. Light the incense.

The Petitioner's Candle stands on the Placket. On the four corners of the Placket rest the four Rubies.

With the Oil, dress the Altar Candles and the Day Candle, while concentrating on the purpose of the ritual.

Light your taper; then from that, light the Altar Candles and the Day Candle. State your intent:

I am here to help [Name] accept [his/her] situation, to understand [his/her] obligations, and to bring about the meeting of those obligations.

With the Awl, inscribe the Petitioner's name on the Astral Candle, and then dress the candle with Oil.

With your taper, light the Petitioner Candle and say:

This is [Name], who has the strength to overcome all adversity. Let [his/her] spirit burn as surely as does this flame; a symbol of the inner strength that will prevail in all matters.

With the Awl, inscribe Gold Candles #1 and #3 with the word "Attraction," and Gold Candles #2 and #4 with the word "Need." Dress them with Oil.

Light the Gold Candles #1 and #3 and say:

Here do I light the first pair of Lamps of Fortune. May their light ease the burden by attracting needed money to the Petitioner.

Light the Gold Candles #2 and #4 and say:

Here do I light the second pair of Lamps of Fortune.
May they, too, ease the financial burden and draw in
the needed money to meet the obligation.

Take up the Censer and swing it, censing the whole area around the altar, while rhythmically repeating the Key Word "Money," and building up the energy to that focus. Replace the Censer and direct your energies toward the Green Candles. Light them in order and say:

Money is all about me. It is ready and waiting to
move in and fill my needs. With the generating of this
psychic power, moneys are being attracted to me. My
financial obligations are being met.

Move Green Candle #1 in toward the center. (Since the ritual is to be done over a period of seven days, *move the candle one-seventh of the distance each day* of the ritual. In this way it will end up against the Petitioner's candle after the seven days.) Now take Ruby #1 and move it out and around the Green #1 Candle, and back to its place on the corner of the Placket (see diagram).

Move Green Candle #2 one-seventh of the way in toward the center. Take Ruby #2 and move it out and around the Green #2 Candle, and back to its place on the corner of the Placket. Repeat with Green Candles #3 and #4, and Rubies #3 and #4. (At this point, on the last day only, when all four Green Candles are tight up

against the Petitioner's candle, again take the Censer
and thoroughly cense the whole set-up while chanting
the Key Word "Money.")

Now sit and meditate on money coming in, and you
paying your debts. Don't stop to rationalize as to where
the money is coming from; just see it pouring in, and
see yourself paying off your debts. Then see yourself
with all your debts paid and you celebrating your new-
found freedom.

Extinguish the candles in the opposite order and
leave set-up, undisturbed, until the next day's ritual.

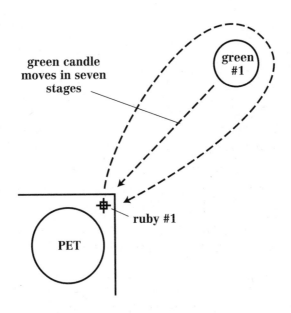

Movement of green candles and rubies.

TO MEET YOUR SPIRIT GUIDE

We each have a Spirit Guide. Some refer to it as a "Guardian Angel" or a "Gate Keeper." Some of us have more than one. When we try to make contact with departed spirits it is our Spirit Guide who makes the connection for us, keeping out those we don't wish to communicate with, and assisting those we do. (See my book *Doors to Other Worlds*, Llewellyn, 1993.)

For some people it is relatively easy to make contact with their Guide, but for others it is not. This ritual will help in clearing the way; will assist in drawing back the veil, so that you may peer into the light.

Timing
Any time, though early morning or late evening hours seem to be best for most people

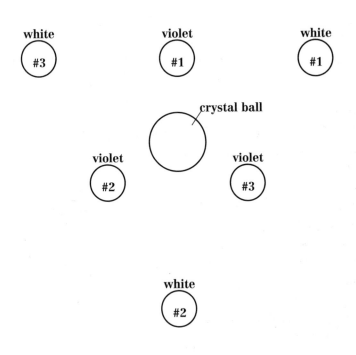

Altar Set-up #9
"To Meet Your Spirit Guide"

Day(s)
Any day

Hour
Mercury

Candles
Day candle as appropriate; Offertory: Violet (3) inscribed
"Spirit," White (3) inscribed "Truth"

Incense
Anise, cardamom, and coriander, or fleawort, hemp
seed, parsley, and violet root

Oil
Acacia, anise, and cassia, or gardenia, jasmine, and
lotus, or jasmine, lemon, rose, and sandalwood

Key Word
"Merge"

Supplementary Items
Crystal ball

Bath
Almond, anise, lavender, mint, and orange bergamot,
or cinnamon, frankincense, myrrh, and sandalwood

Breathe deeply and build your ball of protective light.
While soaking in your ritual bath, meditate on the whole

ritual: the steps you will take and what you wish to say to your Spirit Guide when you make contact. Enter the Circle in the hour of Mercury. Light the incense. With the Oil, dress the Altar Candles and the Day Candle, while concentrating on the purpose of the ritual.

Light your taper; then from that, light the Altar Candles and the Day Candle. State your intent:

I am here to make contact with my Spirit Guide, and to acknowledge him or her.

With the Awl, inscribe the Violet #1 Candle with the word "Spirit." Dress it with Oil.

Light the Violet #1 Candle, direct your energies into it, and say:

Here do I light the first Lamp of Spirit. May its light reach out across the barriers from this world to the next. May it make contact with that World of Spirit into which we will all eventually enter.

Take up the Censer and swing it, censing the whole area around the altar, while rhythmically repeating the Key Word "Merge," and building up the energy to that focus. Replace the Censer and take up the Violet #2 Candle. Inscribe it with the word "Spirit," and dress it with the Oil. Put it back in its place and light it, directing your energies into it. Say:

Here do I light the second Lamp of Spirit. May its light also reach out across the barriers from this world to the next. May it make contact with that World of Spirit and help spread the light, illuminating the passageway between our worlds.

Take up the Censer and again swing it, censing the whole area around the altar, while rhythmically repeating the Key Word "Merge," and building up the energy to that focus. Replace the Censer. Take up the Violet #3 Candle, inscribe it with the word "Spirit," and dress it with Oil. Replace it and light it. Say:

Here do I light the third Lamp of Spirit. May its light also reach out across the barriers from this world to the next. May the light from these three lamps blend and grow, dispelling all darkness and lighting the way that my Spirit Guide may come to me and speak with me here today.

Inscribe each of the three White Candles with the word "Truth," and anoint each with Oil. Light the White #1, #2, and #3 Candles in order saying:

Here do I build Truth. As these candles burn throughout this ritual, their power generates nothing but the truth in all that transpires between this world and the next. Through these candles there is truth in all communications that come to me.

Take up the Censer and again cense the whole ritual area, while chanting the Key Word "Merge." As you finish censing, replace the Censer, but keep up the chanting, sitting, and now gazing into the crystal ball as you chant. (A clear glass tumbler filled to the brim with water will do if you do not have a crystal ball. Stand the ball or glass on a piece of black cloth—velvet is best—so that your eye is not distracted when skrying.) When you feel right, let your chanting taper off until you sit quietly looking into the crystal.

Do not try to picture anything in the crystal. Rather, try to keep your mind blank, so that whatever will come and appear to you comes of its own free will. Gaze into the center of the ball. There is no need to try not to blink; look naturally, blinking as you need, but try not to be distracted. Try not to notice anything in your peripheral vision; just gaze into the center of the ball.

Eventually a face or figure will appear there. It may take a long while to come, or it may appear almost immediately. If it doesn't come at all, after twenty minutes of waiting, abandon this attempt. Extinguish the candles in reverse order to that in which they were lit and, leaving everything set up, leave the ritual area. Try again in three day's time. If nothing happens then, try in three more days, and so on. You should have results within a month at the most.

If a figure does appear, accept it, and ask if he/she is your Spirit Guide. You will hear an answer. You may not hear it out loud, or even see the figure's lips move, but you will become aware of the answer. This is how most of your "conversation" will proceed: you will ask your questions mentally (or out loud) and the answers will come into your head as though you are hearing them from the Spirit Guide.

Ask if you have more than one Spirit Guide and, if you do, ask for them to also appear to you.

You may ask anything you wish, but I would suggest establishing a connection whereby your Guide may appear to you at any time, or at specific times, so that you can converse with other spirits through him/her.

When you have finished speaking with your Guide, thank him/her, and then sit for a moment with your eyes closed, meditating on all you have learned. Extinguish the candles in reverse order.

TO PROTECT FROM ABUSE

It is a sad reflection on modern-day society that abuse is a common problem around the world. Spousal and child abuse have finally been given a prominence by the media that is unprecedented. There is no doubt that abuse has been prevalent for centuries; it's just something that was not to be reported or even mentioned; at last we have found our voice to cry out against this atrocity.

This ritual is one that may be done by a victim of abuse—whatever type—and from it he or she will gain strength and courage to end it, in one way or another. No abuse should go unreported.

Timing
May be done at any time, though if at all possible start on a Tuesday or a Friday

Day(s)
Three consecutive

Hour
Mars

Candles
Astral for Petitioner; Day Candles as appropriate; Offertory: White and Pink (3) inscribed "Love/Purification," Green and Gold (1) inscribed "Healing/Protection"

Incense
Gum Arabic or dragon's blood, frankincense, and sandalwood

Oil
Cypress, rose geranium, and rosemary for White/Pink Candles; ambergris, civet, and lotus for Green/Gold Candles

Key Word
"Freedom-Joy"

Supplementary Items
Opal or jade (3); Wand

Bath
Cinnamon, lavender, and rosemary

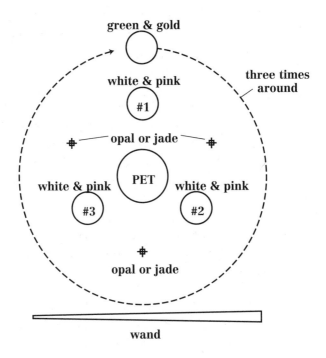

Altar Set-up #10
"To Protect from Abuse"

Breathe deeply and build your ball of protective light. While soaking in your ritual bath, meditate on the whole ritual: the steps you will take leading to being free of the abuse and being happy and joyful. Enter the Circle in the hour of Mars on a Tuesday or Friday if possible (if not, this may be done any day). Light the incense. With the Oil, dress the Altar Candles and the Day Candle, while concentrating on the purpose of the ritual.

Light your taper; then from that, light the Altar Candles and the Day Candle. State your intent:

I am here to help [Name] change [his/her] situation [or "I am here to help change my situation"]; to end the abuse that has been suffered and to allow [him/ her/me] to merge and blend in once more with the pure joy of living.

With the Awl, inscribe the Petitioner's name on the Astral Candle, and then dress the candle with Oil.

With your taper, light the Petitioner Candle and say:

This is [Name], who has the strength to overcome all negativity. Let [his/her] spirit burn as surely as does this flame; a symbol of the inner strength that will prevail in all things.

With the Awl, inscribe the White and Pink #1 Candle with the words "Love" and "Purification." Dress it with Oil.

Light the White and Pink #1 Candle and say:

Here do I light the first beacon in a circle of power encompassing [Name]. As the light builds let [his/ her] strength multiply to overcome what has been suffered. May this light ease the burden placed on [him/her] and open [him/her] once again to the joy of life and of living.

Take up the Censer and swing it, censing the whole area around the altar, while rhythmically repeating the Key Word "Freedom-Joy," and building up the energy to that focus. Replace the Censer and direct your energies toward the White and Pink #2 Candle. Say:

Here do I light the second beacon in a circle of power encompassing [Name]. This light builds the power and increases [his/her] strength to overcome what has been suffered and to accept pure love and joy in all things. May this combined light ease the burden and open [him/her] once again to the joy of life and of living.

Take up the Censer and swing it, censing the whole area around the altar, while rhythmically repeating the Key Word "Freedom-Joy," and building up the energy to that focus. Replace the Censer and direct your energies toward the White and Pink #3 Candle. Say:

Now is the circle of power complete about [Name]. Here burns the flame of right and might, protecting [him/her] and bringing joy and love into [his/her] life once more.

Take up the Wand and touch it to each of the three
Opals (or Jade) in turn. As you touch each Stone see
power and energy coming from the gods into your
body and thence into the wand. Direct that energy into
each stone, seeing it as divine power that purifies and
protects. (Some people see the power from God/God-
dess/All-That-Is coming down from the sky like a beam
of light, and entering the head at the position of the
third eye. Others see the energy coming up from the
ground and rising through the feet and legs into the
body. Visualize whatever is best for you. See Chapter
Six, "Consecration.")

Now, with the Awl, inscribe the Green and Gold Candle with the words "Healing" and "Protection." Dress it
with Oil. Light the Candle and say:

*Here now is Healing and Protection. Never again to
suffer; never again to feel unloved.*

Take the Candle and move it slowly in a clockwise
circle, three times about the center group of candles. As
you move it, concentrate on a life filled with joy and love,
without fear and without suffering. Know that the abuse
will end. Know that the Petitioner's life is going to change
for the better. See it as if it has already happened.

Sit for a few minutes enjoying the new life. Feel the
love and joy that exist in the world, and which are now
a part of the Petitioner. They are his/her right. Then
extinguish the candles in reverse order.

Repeat the ritual for three consecutive days.

Do not entertain thoughts of revenge or retribution toward the abuser. This is not your concern. In Wicca, and many other branches of paganism, it is believed that there is retribution *in this life* and that it is a three-fold retribution. The gods—God/Goddess/All-That-Is—will take care of that. Concentrate your energies on the abused; on returning him/her to health and happiness.

TO PROTECT ON A JOURNEY

Most of us do far more traveling today than our parents ever did, and far and away more than our grandparents ever dreamed of doing. Yet with travel has come danger—hijackings, bombings, muggings, theft. It behooves the wary traveler to take precautions before leaving home.

Timing
In the waxing cycle of the Moon

Day(s)
Wednesday prior to departure

Hour
Mars

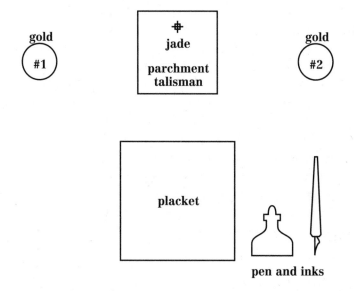

gold
#1

jade

parchment
talisman

gold
#2

placket

pen and inks

Altar Set-up #11
"To Protect on a Journey"

Candles
Day: Purple; Offertory: Gold (2) inscribed "Protection"

Incense
Birch bark, dragon's blood, and juniper or clove, frankincense and myrrh, or copal, dragon's blood, and frankincense

Oil
Cypress, rose geranium, and rosemary or dragon's blood, frankincense, and sandalwood

Key Word
"Safe"

Supplementary Items
Jade (1); Parchment square (approx. 3" x 3"); Pen; Inks (black and purple); Placket (Yellow)

Bath
Cinnamon, lavender, and rosemary

Breathe deeply and build your ball of protective light. While soaking in your ritual bath, meditate on the whole ritual: the steps you will take and the end you have in mind—safety throughout your journeys. Enter the Circle in the hour of Mars on a Wednesday, in the waxing cycle of the Moon closest to the start of your traveling. Light the incense. With the Oil, dress the Altar Candles and the Day Candle, while concentrating on the purpose of the ritual.

Light your taper; then from that, light the Altar Candles and the Day Candle. State your intent:

I am here to enclose [Name] with protection that will envelope [him/her] like a cocoon throughout [his/her] journeys; from the time of leaving home until the time of safe return.

With the Awl, inscribe the Gold #1 and #2 Candles with the word "Protection." Anoint them with Oil. With your taper, light the two Gold Candles and say:

Here burns the golden light of protection, shining all around [Name]. [He/she] is totally enclosed in the light. It burns with a fierce strength that cannot be overcome.

Take up the Censer and swing it, censing the whole area around the altar, while rhythmically repeating the Key Word "Safe," and building up the energy to that focus. Replace the Censer.

In the light of the two Gold Candles, make a talisman for safety from the parchment (see Chapter Five). Use black ink for marking the squares, and purple for the letters or characters. Use whichever Magickal Alphabet you prefer. Make the Magickal Square for Protection:

<pre>
A   M   P   A
R   O   L   A
M   P   A   R
O   L   A   M
</pre>

Help the ink to dry by holding the talisman near the candle flames. Then hold it in the smoke of the incense and say:

Here have I created a Talisman of Protection. By the sacred forces contained in it, [Name] will be safe from all harm for as long as [he/she] may journey. This parchment will shield and protect from any and all harm, damage, and disaster.

Replace the talisman between the Gold Candles, and take up the Jade in your right hand (left, if left-handed). Hold it over your heart and say:

This sacred Stone is the very essence of safety, guarding and protecting its owner wherever he/she may go. The pulse of the gem blends now with the pulse of the heart so that the two beat as one.

Hold it for a while, then wrap the Jade in the parchment Talisman and place it in the Placket. Carry the Placket with you throughout your journeys.

When you feel ready, extinguish the candles in reverse order.

TO REACH A DECISION

It's not always easy to make a decision. Sometimes the choices can be so overwhelming that we keep turning them over and over in our minds until we just don't know what to do. The first thing to do is to sit down and list the various choices; actually write them down. Then, under each one, make two columns: one giving the advantages of going with that choice and the other the disadvantages. Many times just putting things down on paper, so that you can look at them and compare them, helps you make the choice; but for when there is still confusion, try this Candle Magick ritual.

Timing
New Moon

Day(s)
Sunday

Hour
Jupiter

Candles
Astral for Petitioner; Day: Yellow; Offertory: Red (2) inscribed "Courage"

Incense
Chicory, cinquefoil, and clove or benzoin, pepperwort, and wood aloes or cinnamon, citron peel, clove, lemon balm, and nutmeg

Oil
Cinnamon, clove, and nutmeg, or one drop of clove oil in three ounces of olive oil, with a little red coloring

Key Word
"Decision"

Supplementary Items
Mirror; Paper (as many pieces as there are possible choices, each piece approximately 3" x 3"); Pen and Ink; Dish

Bath
Cypress, honeysuckle, magnolia, and patchouli or frankincense, rose geranium, and rosemary

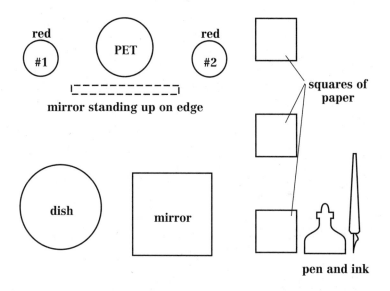

Altar Set-up #12
"To Reach a Decision"

Breathe deeply and build your ball of protective light. While soaking in your ritual bath, meditate on the decision to be made, and who and what will be affected by the different decisions possible. Enter the Circle in the hour of Jupiter on the Sunday closest to the New Moon. Stand, kneel, or sit before the altar. Light the incense. With the Oil, dress the Altar Candles and the Day Candle, while concentrating on the purpose of the ritual.

Light your taper; then from that, light the Altar Candles and the Day Candle. State your intent:

I am here to help [Name] make a wise and just decision; a decision which will have no adverse effect on anyone.

With the Awl, inscribe the Petitioner's name on the Astral Candle, then dress the candle with Oil. With your taper, light the Petitioner Candle and say:

This is [Name], who has the strength to make a decision and the wisdom to make a wise decision. Let [his/her] spirit burn as surely as does this flame; a symbol of that inner strength and wisdom that will prevail in all things.

With the Awl, inscribe the Red #1 and #2 Candles with the word "Courage." Dress them with Oil.
Light the Red #1 Candle and say:

Here do I light the first Lamp of Courage. May its light ease the burden of decision-making.

Light the Red #2 Candle and say:

Here do I light the second Lamp of Courage. May its
light show the way toward a fair and just decision.

Take up the Censer and swing it, censing the whole
area around the altar, while rhythmically repeating the
Key Word "Decision," and building up the energy to that
focus. Replace the Censer.

Take up the Mirror and hold it in the smoke of the
Censer, saying:

Here is the Mirror of Decision. Reflection can lead to
wise choices. In that sense, let me use the reflection
of this Mirror to arrive at a sure and just decision.

Stand the Mirror on its edge so that it rests against,
and is held upright by, the Petitioner's Candle.

With Pen and Ink, write the main points of each of
the possible decisions, one on each piece of paper, your
mind focusing on the fact that a just decision will be
made. Roll up the pieces of paper into little balls, and
hold them in your cupped hands. Hold your hands over
the incense. Say:

Here lie the decisions. One of these is the correct one.
Now do I draw on the courage that burns bravely on
either side of me, that I may make the right decision.

Throw the wadded balls of Paper at the Mirror with
sufficient force that they strike the face of the Mirror

and bounce back to land on the altar top between you and the Mirror. One ball of Paper will be closer to you than the others. (If more than one are equidistant from the Mirror, then throw those again until just one is closer to you than all the others. If, on the first throw, one of the papers misses the mirror then throw them all again.) The ball closest to you is the best decision. Open it and read it. Then take all the balls of Paper and place them in the dish, and set fire to them with the taper. Make sure they burn to ashes.

Sit for a moment and contemplate what you have done. Think no more of the possibilities; only know that the decision you have made is the right one.

Extinguish the candles in reverse order.

TO RELEASE

This is a cleansing ritual. It is something that will be found to be extremely useful when trying to get over the trauma of abuse or of a rape, the agony of a divorce or separation, or the frustration of being fired from a job. It helps release all the pent-up feelings; all the negativity and potential self-destruction.

Timing
In the waning cycle of the Moon

Day(s)
Three consecutive Sundays (the first two, at least, should fall into the waning cycle)

Hour
Moon

Candles
Astral for Petitioner; Day: Yellow; Offertory: White (2) inscribed "Purity," Red (2) one inscribed "Courage" and one inscribed "Strength," Greenish/Yellow (4) inscribed "Discord," Green (4) inscribed "Healing"

Incense
Gum Arabic or frankincense or juniper

Oil
Gardenia, rose, and tuberose or frankincense, myrrh, olive, and sandalwood for White Candles and Red Candles; cinnamon, clove, and benzoin for Green Candles

Key Word
"Purify"

Bath
Basil, cumin, rosemary, and yarrow or basil, fennel, hyssop, lavender, mint, rosemary, thyme, valerian, and vervain

Breathe deeply and build your ball of protective light. While soaking in your ritual bath, meditate on the whole ritual. Do not dwell on the hurt you have suffered, but think, rather, of releasing it, and of enjoying the peace and purity of spiritual recleansing. Enter the Circle in the hour of the Moon on the first Sunday. Stand, kneel, or sit before the altar. Light the incense. With the Oil, dress the

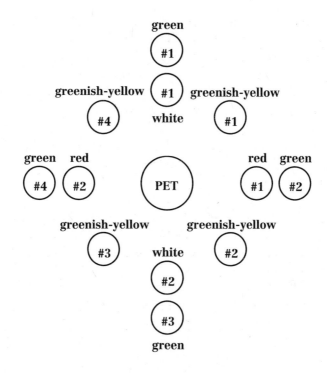

Altar Set-up #13
"To Release"

Altar Candles and the Day Candle, while concentrating on the purpose of the ritual.

Light your taper; then from that, light the Altar Candles and the Day Candle. State your intent:

I am here to help [Name] come to terms with an unhappy chapter in [his/her] life; to release the hurt and to put the past behind [him/her]; to rekindle the flame of love and pleasure, looking forward to opportunities that are offered, and to all that life holds for [him/her] in the future.

With the Awl, inscribe the Petitioner's name on the Astral Candle, then dress the candle with Oil.

With your taper, light the Petitioner Candle and say:

This is [Name], who has the strength to overcome all negativity. Let [his/her] spirit burn as surely as does this flame; a symbol of the inner strength that will prevail in all things.

With the Awl, inscribe the White #1 and #2 Candles with the word "Purity." Dress them with Oil, then light them and say:

Here do I light the Twin Pillars of Purity. May the light here generated spread around [him/her] and throughout [him/her].

With the Awl, inscribe the Red #1 Candle with the word "Strength," and the Red #2 Candle with the word "Courage." Dress them with Oil, then light them and say:

Here burns the Strength and Courage that is needed to turn from the negative to the positive. Let that strength be here, as these flames burn, and let it permeate all that it touches, giving the fortitude to move on through life, leaving negativity behind.

With the Awl, inscribe the four Greenish-Yellow Candles with the word "Discord." Dress them with Oil, then light them and say:

Here burns Discord. Here stands the misery that is now suppressed. Here past deeds smolder and flame, their time now limited.

Take up the Censer and swing it, censing the whole area around the altar, while rhythmically repeating the Key Word "Purify," and building up the energy to that focus. Replace the Censer.

With the Awl, inscribe the Green #1, #2, #3, and #4 Candles with the word "Healing." Dress them with Oil.

Taking the Greenish-Yellow #1 Candle with your right hand and the Green #1 Candle with your left hand, change their places (see diagram), moving them in a counterclockwise direction, so that the Green Candle is now between White #1 and Red #1. Do the same with Greenish-Yellow #2 and Green #2, Greenish-Yellow #3 and Green #3, and Greenish-Yellow #4 and Green #4.

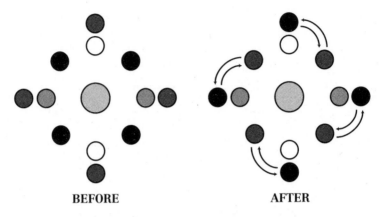

BEFORE   **AFTER**

Movement of the green and greenish-yellow candles.

Now, with the taper, light the four Green Candles and say:

> *Healing burns as steadily as do these flames. Healing burns away all negativity and hurt, leaving behind nothing but strength and love. Healing is the gift of the gods and soothes away all pain. Let these four healing flames encircle and revive, mend and restore. Now can nothing reach [Name] but goodness and purity. All will be well!*

Again cense the whole area, chanting "Purify." Then sit and concentrate your thoughts on a new life ahead, filled with love and golden opportunities.

Extinguish the candles in the opposite order to the way in which they were lit. On the following Sunday, start again with the candles in their original positions, so that the ritual may be done the same way.

TO START A NEW VENTURE

Whether it be starting a new job, opening a business, starting a new life as a married person, or newly divorced, leaving your parents' home to be on your own, emigrating to a new land, being initiated into a new or different religion, there are many and various ways that some of us start new ventures. Here is a ritual that can make the transition go smoothly.

Timing
For seven days during the waxing cycle of the Moon

Day(s)
Saturday, Sunday, Monday, Tuesday, Wednesday, Thursday, Friday

Hour
Mercury

Candles
Astral for Petitioner; Day Candles as appropriate; Offertory: Brown (1) inscribed "Neutral," Yellow (1) inscribed "Confidence," Orange (1) inscribed "Encouragement," White (1) inscribed "Truth"

Incense
Myrrh or birch bark, dragon's blood, and juniper, or gum Arabic, lavender, and sandalwood

Oil
Cinnamon, myrtle, and olive oil for Brown Candle; cinnamon, clove, mace, narcissus, and storax, or cinnamon and patchouli for all others

Key Word
"Success"

Bath
Jasmine, lemon, lotus, and sandalwood

Breathe deeply and build your ball of protective light. While soaking in your ritual bath, meditate on the venture you are about to undertake. See it as a wonderful golden road stretching out before you, with incredible opportunities and the promise of great rewards. Enter the Circle in the hour of Mercury on a

Altar Set-up #14
"To Start a New Venture"

Saturday in the waxing cycle of the Moon. Stand, kneel, or sit before the altar. Light the incense. With the Oil, dress the Altar Candles and the Day Candle, while concentrating on the purpose of the ritual.

Light your taper; then from that, light the Altar Candles and the Day Candle. State your intent:

> *I am here to help [Name] set out upon a new road; a road to success. Here starts a new and exciting venture filled with opportunity. Let there be no regrets for the past as [he/she] faces the future, secure in the knowledge that all will go well.*

With the Awl, inscribe the Petitioner's name on the Astral Candle, then dress the candle with Oil.

With your taper, light the Petitioner Candle and say:

> *This is [Name], who has the strength to overcome all negativity as [he/she] sets out to build a new life filled with promise. Let [his/her] spirit burn as surely as does this flame; a symbol of the inner strength that will prevail in all things.*

With the Awl, inscribe the Brown Candle with the word "Neutral." Dress it with Oil and say:

> *Here do I light the Lamp of Neutrality. This represents the past. Let the past be neutral so far as it affects the future, for here is the start of a new venture.*

With the Awl, inscribe the Yellow candle with the word "Confidence." Dress it with Oil, light it and say:

Here burns the confidence which [Name] has in [him/herself]. With a new purpose to life there is joy and determination. This flame burns steadily, reflecting that confidence.

With the Awl, inscribe the Orange candle with the word "Encouragement." Dress it with Oil, light it and say:

Encouragement burns ahead, drawing [him/her] forward to better and greater things. Anything is possible if you have the courage to try it. Encouragement is all you need and it is here in abundance.

With the Awl, inscribe the White candle with the word "Truth." Dress it with Oil, light it and say:

Truth is the light at the end of the tunnel. It burns for all to see. It is the foundation on which to build any new venture. Here it is in its rightful place as a part of what may be achieved. Truth burns brightly and strongly.

Take up the Censer and swing it, censing the whole area around the altar, while rhythmically repeating the Key Word "Success," and building up the energy to that focus. Replace the Censer. Say:

Now does [Name] set off on [his/her] new venture, steady in the knowledge that all will go well. [His/ hers] is the path that leads to success.

Slowly move the Petitioner's Candle one-seventh of the way toward the Yellow, White, and Orange Candles, and say:

The way to success is straight and true, lined with opportunity and edged with love. Every step of the way [his/her] progress is watched over, each and every move planned for only good. Let the journey be enjoyed as it brings love and good fellowship into the way of the traveler. Start the new venture and enjoy the journey!

Sit for a while and picture the venture well under way, and bringing great joy and pleasure to the Petitioner. See him/her with no cares or worries, enjoying life to the fullest.

Extinguish the candles in reverse order and leave them in their positions. Start from those positions the next day, so that the Petitioner's Candle will be moved another seventh of the way to the right. In this way, by the end of the week it will meet, and touch, the Yellow, White, and Orange Candles.

TO STOP A BAD HABIT

Whether it be smoking, drinking, nail-biting, or putting the phrase "you know" into every sentence uttered, many of us have what can only be called bad habits that we would be far better off without. If we are able to acknowledge these bad habits, that's half the battle; but to then actually take steps to get rid of them can be far from easy. Here is a ritual that can help you focus on what you want to achieve, and which will Magickally aid you in getting rid of the bad habit.

Timing
To be started in the waning cycle of the Moon and repeated every Monday for seven weeks

Day(s)
Monday

Hour
Moon

Candles
Astral for Petitioner; Day: White; Offertory: Light Blue
(3) inscribed "Patience," Green (3) inscribed "Health"

Incense
Bay or thyme or juniper berries and rosemary

Oil
Cinnamon, myrtle, and olive or carnation, rosemary,
and sandalwood

Key Word
"No more"

Supplementary Items
Poppet stuffed with verbena (vervain) and cloves;
Brown wool or brown silk ribbon (21" long); Dish

Bath
Frankincense, rose geranium, and rosemary or clove,
frankincense, rosemary, and sandalwood

The Poppet, representing the Petitioner, should be
made ahead of time as described in Chapter Five, and
stuffed with verbena and cloves.

Breathe deeply and build your ball of protective
light. While soaking in your ritual bath, meditate on the

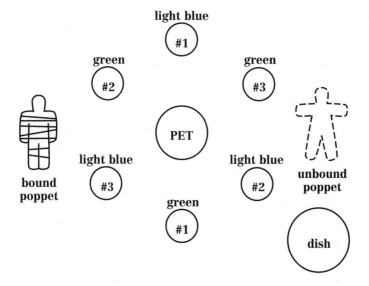

Altar Set-up #15
"To Stop a Bad Habit"

whole ritual, concentrating on being free of the bad habit. Enter the Circle in the hour of the Moon on the first Monday and stand, kneel, or sit before the altar. Light the incense. With the Oil, dress the Altar Candles and the Day Candle, while concentrating on the purpose of the ritual.

Light your taper; then from that, light the Altar Candles and the Day Candle. State your intent:

I am here to help [Name] overcome a bad habit; to gain full control of [his/her] life and to live it to the full, with love and enjoyment.

With the Awl, inscribe the Petitioner's name on the Astral Candle, then dress the candle with Oil.

With your taper, light the Petitioner Candle and say:

This is [Name], who has the strength to overcome all negativity. Let [his/her] spirit burn as surely as does this flame; a symbol of the inner strength that will prevail in all things.

Take up the Censer and swing it, censing the whole area around the altar, while rhythmically repeating the Key Words "No more!" and building up the energy to that focus. Replace the Censer. Take up the Poppet and hold it in the smoke of the Censer. Say:

I name this Poppet [Name]. It is [him/her] in every way. Anything I do to this Poppet I do to [him/her].

With the length of Wool or ribbon, bind the Poppet, tying its arms and legs tightly to the body. Again hold the Poppet in the smoke of the incense. Say:

Here is [Name] as [he/she] is now; bound by a habit that [he/she] would break. As time passes, the bonds will fall away and [he/she] will be free.

Place the Poppet on the left side of the candles.

With the Awl, inscribe the Light Blue #1 Candle with the word "Patience." Dress it with Oil.

Light the Light Blue #1 Candle and say:

Here do I light the first Lamp of Patience, knowing that a long-held habit cannot be broken overnight. May this light ease the burden of the habit that is still strong.

With the Awl, inscribe the Green #1 Candle with the word "Health." Dress it with Oil.

Light the Green #1 Candle and say:

Here is the Health that will be improving as the habit is lost. It will grow and burn steadily as the flame, bringing peace and joy to [Name].

With the Awl, inscribe the Light Blue #2 Candle with the word "Patience." Dress it with Oil.

Light the Light Blue #2 Candle and say:

Here do I light the second Lamp of Patience, knowing that a long-held habit cannot be broken overnight. May this light add to the first and ease the burden of the habit that is still strong.

With the Awl, inscribe the Green #2 Candle with the word "Health." Dress it with Oil.

Light the Green #2 Candle and say:

Here is the Health that will be improving as the habit is lost. It will grow and burn steadily as these flames, bringing peace and joy to [Name].

With the Awl, inscribe the Light Blue #3 Candle with the word "Patience." Dress it with Oil.

Light the Light Blue #3 Candle and say:

Here do I light the third Lamp of Patience, knowing that a long-held habit cannot be broken overnight. May these three lights ease the burden of the habit that is still strong.

With the Awl, inscribe the Green #3 Candle with the word "Health." Dress it with Oil.

Light the Green #3 Candle and say:

Here is the total Health that improves as the habit flees. It grows and burns steadily, bringing peace and joy to [Name].

Take up the Censer and swing it, again censing the whole area around the altar, while rhythmically repeating the Key Words "No more!" and building up the energy to that focus. Replace the Censer.

Sit quietly in meditation, seeing the Petitioner free of the habit and living happily in love and enjoyment. Extinguish the candles in reverse order.

For the following weeks, repeat the ritual leaving the Poppet bound, on the left side of the candles, as it was after the first time through the ritual. Simply repeat the section as follows:

Hold the Poppet in the smoke of the incense. Say:

Here is [Name] as [he/she] is now; bound by a habit that [he/she] would break. As time passes the bonds will fall away and [he/she] will be free.

Lay the Poppet on the left of the candles.

On the final week, repeat the ritual, but when you light the Light Blue #3 Candle, say:

Here do I light the third Lamp of Patience knowing that the long-held habit of [Name] is finally broken. May the light from these lamps shine forward on a life of love and joy.

Take up the Poppet and unbind it. Say:

Here once again is [Name], now free and unencumbered. The habit has gone and life is full and happy once again.

Lay the ribbon/wool in the dish and burn it.

With the Awl, inscribe the Green #3 Candle with the word "Health." Dress it with Oil.

Light the Green #3 Candle and say:

Here is the total Health now complete and whole. The habit is fled; gone never to return. As these candles burn steadily, so is [Name's] life steady and robust, with peace, joy, and love.

Take up the Censer and cense the entire area. Sit quietly and contemplate life without the habit, knowing it to be full, healthy, and happy. Extinguish the candles in reverse order.

FOR PURIFICATION

Various Native American peoples have sweat lodges which they use for purification rites. In Polynesia and Micronesia, purification is obtained through the use of fire and water. In India, bathing in the river Ganges, with devotions to the goddess Ganga, is the Hindu way of cleansing and purifying. With the African Kikuyu, it involves drinking a potion containing undigested food from the stomach of a sacrificial goat or lamb. Many other cultures have special rites with various ritual methods of purification.

The need for purification may be brought about by laws of the religious or ethnic group in which you live, but frequently the need is simply felt by the individual. This is especially true when that individual feels as though he or she has been violated in some way. Here is a ritual to bring about that purification.

Timing
To be done during the waning cycle of the Moon

Day(s)
Monday, Tuesday, and Friday

Hour
Venus

Candles
Astral for Petitioner; Day candles as appropriate; Offertory: White (5) inscribed "Purify"

Incense
Cinnamon and sandalwood, or frankincense and vervain

Oil
Frankincense, myrrh, olive, and sandalwood

Key Word
"Purify"

Supplementary Items
Poppet stuffed with fennel, mugwort (or St. John's Wort), and plantain; five precious/semi-precious stones: amethyst, bloodstone, peridot, ruby, and pink/green tourmaline

Bath
Frankincense, rose geranium, and rosemary

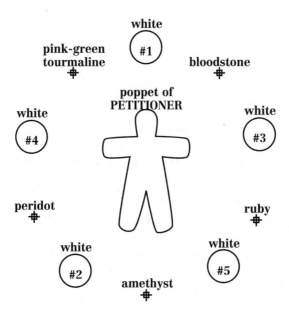

Altar Set-up #16
"For Purification"

The Poppet, representing the Petitioner, should be made ahead of time as described in Chapter Five, and stuffed with fennel, mugwort (or St. John's wort), and plantain. The five Stones lie on the left of the altar at the start of the ritual, and may be placed around the Poppet when instructed.

Breathe deeply and build your ball of protective light. While soaking in your ritual bath, meditate on the reasons for needing purification, knowing that with this ritual you will be able to put all negativity behind you and once more enjoy life. Enter the Circle in the hour of Venus on Monday, and stand, kneel, or sit before the altar. Light the incense. With the Oil, dress the Altar Candles and the Day Candle, while concentrating on the purpose of the ritual.

Light your taper; then from that, light the Altar Candles and the Day Candle. State your intent:

I am here to cleanse and purify myself; to obliterate the negativity of the past and to welcome the love and joy of the future.

Take up the Poppet and hold it in the smoke of the incense. Say:

This is me, [Name], who has the strength to overcome all negativity. I am now filled with the healing powers of the herbs, and filled, spiritually, with the healing powers of the Magick conjured here. Bright forces are at work to cleanse and purify me, and to set my feet once more on a positive path toward joy and love.

With the Awl, inscribe the White #1 Candle with the word "Purify." Dress it with Oil.

Light the White #1 Candle and say:

Here do I light the first Lamp of Purification. May its light ease the burden that I bear.

Take up the Censer and swing it, censing the whole area around the altar, while rhythmically repeating the Key Word "Purify," and building up the energy to that focus. Replace the Censer.

With the Awl, inscribe the White #2 Candle with the word "Purify." Dress it with Oil.

Light the White #2 Candle and say:

Here do I light the second Lamp of Purification, knowing that my strength grows as the flames burn.

Take up the Censer and swing it, censing the whole area around the altar, while rhythmically repeating the Key Word "Purify," and building up the energy to that focus. Replace the Censer.

With the Awl, inscribe the White #3 Candle with the word "Purify." Dress it with Oil.

Light the White #3 Candle and say:

Here do I light the third Lamp of Purification. I feel the strength build about me and absorb it into myself.

Take up the Censer and swing it, censing the whole area around the altar, while rhythmically repeating the Key Word "Purify," and building up the energy to that focus. Replace the Censer.

With the Awl, inscribe the White #4 Candle with the word "Purify." Dress it with Oil.

Light the White #4 Candle and say:

Here do I light the fourth Lamp of Purification. Time is the great healer and love is the medicine. Let these flames of love and purity fill my body with the knowledge that I am cleansed.

Take up the Censer and swing it, censing the whole area around the altar, while rhythmically repeating the Key Word "Purify," and building up the energy to that focus. Replace the Censer.

With the Awl, inscribe the White #5 Candle with the word "Purify." Dress it with Oil.

Light the White #5 Candle and say:

Here do I light the final Lamp of Purification. Now do I know that I am loved, for I again have love for myself. As these flames burn strongly and true, so do my body and my spirit burn with an intensity of goodness, love, and purity. I am cleansed and I am born once more into a world of joy.

Take up the Censer and swing it, censing the whole area around the altar, while rhythmically repeating the

Key Word "Purify," and building up the energy to that focus. Replace the Censer.

Take up the five Stones in your left hand (right, if left-handed), and hold them in the smoke of the incense, chanting the Key Word "Purify." Place the Amethyst opposite the White #1 Candle (see diagram) and say:

Here do I surround myself with healing and protection.

Place the Bloodstone opposite the White #2 Candle and say;

Here do I reduce my emotional and mental stress; healing my psyche.

Place the Peridot opposite the White #3 Candle. Say:

Here do I purify myself and increase my psychic awareness.

Place the Ruby opposite the White #4 Candle. Say:

Here do I regenerate myself, filling my body with love and purpose.

Place the Tourmaline opposite the White #5 Candle and say:

Regeneration, balance, harmony, love, and protection are all about me. Now I can look to the future with no further thoughts of the past. Now I can work toward my life goals, knowing that all negativity has been erased. Love and joy are my companions and everything good is my life.

Take up the Censer, and once again cense the whole area, chanting the Key Word "Purify." Set down the Censer and meditate for as long as you need on the future. Give no further thought to the past.

Extinguish the candles in reverse order.

FOR A BIRTH
(Celebration Ritual)

Timing
To be done in the waxing cycle on the Friday closest to
(and before) the Full Moon

Day(s)
Friday

Hour
Moon

Candles
Astral for Petitioner (the newly born); Day: Green; Offertory: White (3) inscribed "Purity," "Truth," "Sincerity"

Incense
Thyme, patchouli, and pine or basil, bergamot, lavender oil, rose petals, and sandalwood

Oil
Cinnamon, frankincense, myrrh, and sandalwood or gardenia, jasmine, and lotus

Key Word
"Beginnings"

Supplementary Items
Precious or semi-precious Stones (7): red, orange, yellow, green, blue, indigo, violet

Bath
Frankincense, rose geranium, and rosemary

Breathe deeply and build your ball of protective light. While soaking in your ritual bath, meditate on the whole miracle of birth, and on the wonderful opportunities that lie ahead for the child. Enter the Circle in the hour of the Moon on the Friday before the Full Moon. Stand, kneel, or sit before the altar. Light the incense. With the Oil, dress the Altar Candles and the Day Candle, while concentrating on the purpose of the ritual.

Light your taper; then from that, light the Altar Candles and the Day Candle. State your intent:

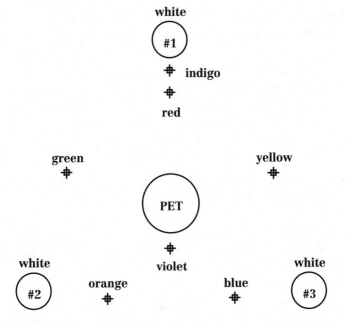

Altar Set-up #17
"For a Birth"

I am here to celebrate the start of a new life; that of [Child's Name]. Through the agencies of God/Goddess/All-That-Is a new creature is among us. Let us welcome [him/her] and cover [him/her] with love.

With the Awl, inscribe the Child's name on the Petitioner Candle, and then dress the candle with Oil.

With your taper, light the Petitioner Candle and say:

This is [Name], a newcomer to our world. Let [his/her] spirit burn as surely as does this flame; a symbol of the inner strength that will prevail throughout [his/her] life in all things.

With the Awl, inscribe the White #1 Candle with the word "Purity." Dress it with Oil.

Light the White #1 Candle and say:

Here do I light the first Lamp of Guardianship. It is the Lamp of Purity. May its light shine throughout the life of this new person, guarding and guiding [him/her] in all things.

Inscribe the White #2 Candle with the word "Truth." Dress it with Oil. Light it and say:

Here do I light the second Lamp of Guardianship. It is the Lamp of Truth. May its light join with Purity to sweep away all darkness and deception from this day forth.

Inscribe the White #3 Candle with the word "Sincerity." Dress it with Oil. Light it and say:

Here do I light the third Lamp of Guardianship. It is the Lamp of Sincerity. May it shine forth in all things connected with this child, to the end of [his/her] days.

Take up the Censer and swing it, censing the whole area around the altar, while rhythmically repeating the Key Word "Beginnings," and building up the energy to that focus. Replace the Censer and take up the seven Stones. Hold them in your cupped hands over the incense and say:

The Seven Sacred Stones of Life shall encircle this newborn child. They will protect [him/her] throughout the long journey from here to death. From each one of these Stones [he/she] may draw strength when needed, each special in its own particular field. The entire spectrum of life is covered by these sacred gems. Let [him/her] be wanting for nothing.

Holding the Stones in your left hand (right, if left-handed), with your other hand take out the Red Stone and lay it down above the Petitioner Candle. Then take the Orange Stone and lay it to the lower left. Then the Yellow Stone to the top right, Green to the top left, Blue to the lower right, Indigo just above the Red Stone, and the Violet at the bottom (just touching) of the Petitioner Candle. In this way you have drawn a pentagram, com-

pleted it, and gone to its center; the Six Points of Magick
(see diagram).

Take up the Censer and again cense the whole area,
chanting "Beginnings," and picturing wonderful opportunities opening up throughout the child's coming life.
Replace the Censer, sit, and meditate further on the life
to be. Extinguish the candles in reverse order. Give the
Stones to the child or to the child's parents.

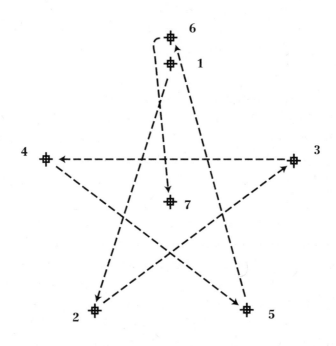

Order for placing stones.

FOR A DEATH
(Celebration Ritual)

Timing
On the night of the New Moon

Hour
Moon

Candles
Astral for Petitioner (the deceased); Day Candle as appropriate; Offertory: Light Blue (4) inscribed "Understanding," Violet (4) inscribed "Peace"

Incense
Frankincense, lavender, and myrrh, or frankincense, mullein, and mimosa, or benzoin, frankincense, myrrh, rosemary, and sandalwood

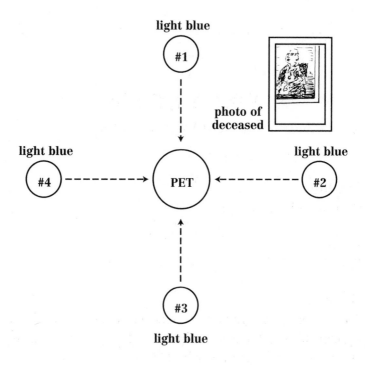

Movement of light blue candles

Altar Set-up #18
"For a Death"

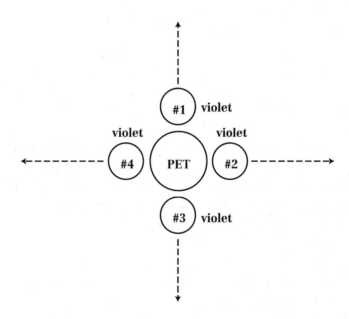

Movement of violet candles

Altar Set-up #18
"For a Death"

Oil
Jasmine, rose, and sandalwood, or frankincense, myrrh, olive, and sandalwood

Key Word
"New Beginnings"

Supplementary Items
Photograph of deceased

Bath
Catnip, elder, hops, and jasmine

Breathe deeply and build your ball of protective light. While soaking in your ritual bath, meditate on the whole life of the deceased remembering, especially, the happy times. Enter the Circle in the hour of the Moon on the night of the New Moon. Stand, kneel, or sit before the altar.

Light the incense. With the Oil, dress the Altar Candles and the Day Candle, while concentrating on the purpose of the ritual.

Light your taper; then from that, light the Altar Candles and the Day Candle. State your intent:

I am here to honor the death of a dear one; to celebrate [his/her] passing-on from this plane of existence to the next.

With the Awl, inscribe the deceased's name on the Petitioner's Candle, and then dress the candle with Oil.

Take up the Photograph and study it for a few moments, reviewing all that you knew of the Deceased, and joining your love and strength with his/hers. If others have sent their love to join with you and the Deceased, then see that all coming together, surrounding the figure in the Photograph. Hold the Photograph in the smoke of the incense for a moment, concentrating on the Key Words "New Beginnings," then set down the Photograph to the right and above the Petitioner Candle.

With your taper, light the Petitioner Candle and say:

This is [Name], who had the courage to fight against all negativity. Let [his/her] spirit burn as surely as does this flame; a symbol of [his/her] inner strength and peace. Let [him/her] move on smoothly to the next plane of existence, to carry out [his/her] appointed tasks.

With the Awl, inscribe all four of the Light Blue Candles with the word "Understanding." Dress them with Oil.

Light the Light Blue #1, #2, #3, and #4 Candles. Say:

Here do I light the Fires of Tranquility, Patience, Peace, and Understanding. May the light from these flames reach across time and space, embracing the light of all knowledge.

Take up the Censer and swing it, censing the whole area around the altar, while rhythmically repeating the Key Words "New Beginnings," and building up the energy to that focus. Replace the Censer. Say:

When the spirit leaves the body and soars to the light, it finds release from all that weighed it down in this life. Behind it, it leaves pain and suffering, want and desire, need and conflict. Ahead lie the Elysium Fields; the land of contentment and happiness. Let us rejoice that a spirit we knew and loved has completed its time on Earth, and returned to the One Home of us all. Understanding has filled the spirit, and now it can move on.

Slowly move the Light Blue #1 Candle in toward the Petitioner's Candle until it touches. Then move the Light Blue #2 in to touch, followed by the Light Blue #3, and the Light Blue #4 (see diagram). When all are touching, extinguish the four flames (not the Petitioner's flame).

Take up the Violet #1 Candle and inscribe it with the word "Peace." Anoint it and then exchange it with Light Blue #1, removing the Light Blue Candle from the altar. Similarly, inscribe and anoint the Violet #2, #3, and #4, and let them replace the other Light Blue candles (see diagram). Light the four Violet Candles and say:

Here now burns the Spirit of Peace. Gone are the trials and tribulations of the flesh as our loved one passes into the light and becomes one with God/Goddess/All-That-Is. From here will [he/she] move on outward, when the time comes, to even better things.

Slowly move the Violet #1 Candle out and away from the Petitioner's Candle (see diagram). Then move out the Violet #2, #3, and #4, until all are at the extremes of the altar.

Take up the Censer and cense the whole altar top while chanting the Key Words "New Beginnings." Set down the Censer.

Sit and meditate on the deceased as you knew him/her best. Know that he/she is happy, and is moving on as was always planned. Know that in time you will meet again and become as one.

Extinguish the candles in reverse order.

FOR PUBERTY
(Celebration Ritual)

Many people celebrate the time of "becoming a man"
or "becoming a woman." It is certainly an important
turning point in one's life. Here is a simple ritual that
the person concerned—the "Pubescent"—may use for
his/her own private celebration.

Timing
In the waxing cycle of the Moon

Day(s)
Friday

Hour
Sun for male; Moon for female

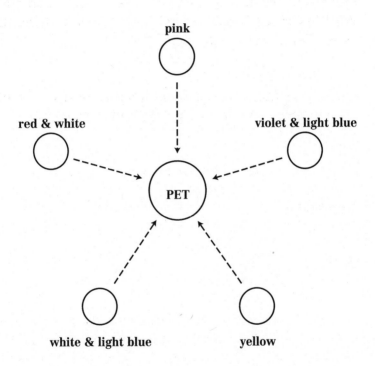

Altar Set-up #19
"For Puberty"

Candles
Astral for Petitioner; Day: Green; Offertory: Pink
inscribed "Love" and "Honor," White and Light Blue
inscribed "Truth" and "Patience," Violet and Light Blue
inscribed "Spirituality" and "Understanding," Red and
White inscribed "Health" and "Purity," Yellow inscribed
"Wisdom" and "Confidence"

Incense
Carnation, frankincense, and juniper, or cinnamon,
frankincense, myrrh, rose petals, and vervain

Oil
Cinnamon, musk, and olive oil

Key Word
"Rebirth"

Bath
Camphor, coconut, lavender, and sweet pea

Breathe deeply and build your ball of protective
light. While soaking in your ritual bath, meditate on the
changes that are taking place in your body. Enter the
Circle in the correct hour of Friday and stand, kneel, or
sit before the altar. Light the incense. With the Oil, dress
the Altar Candles and the Day Candle, while concentrating on the purpose of the ritual.

Light your taper; then from that, light the Altar
Candles and the Day Candle. State your intent:

I am here to celebrate my maturity; my growth from child to adult. I am here to celebrate life and all that it brings.

With the Awl, inscribe the Petitioner's (your) name on the Astral Candle and then dress the candle with Oil. With your taper, light the Petitioner Candle and say:

This is me, [Name], who has grown from baby through child to adult. Within me I have the strength to over- come all negativity. Let my spirit always burn as surely as does this flame. Let me develop wisdom, patience, and understanding. Let me always strive for the truth and never forget my spirituality. Let love fill my life, and let me always send out love to all about me.

With the Awl, inscribe the Pink Candle with the words "Love" and "Honor." Dress it with Oil.

Light the Pink Candle and slowly move it inward to finally touch the Petitioner Candle, saying:

Here Love and Honor move in to become a part of me. Let them become one with me so that I will never forget them.

With the Awl, inscribe the White and Light Blue Candle with the words "Truth" and "Patience." Dress it with Oil. Light the White and Light Blue Candle, and slowly move it inward to finally touch the Petitioner Candle, saying:

Here Truth and Patience move in to become a part of me. Let them become one with me so that I will never forget them.

With the Awl, inscribe the Violet and Light Blue Candle with the words "Spirituality" and "Understanding." Dress it with Oil. Light the Violet and Light Blue Candle, and slowly move it inward to finally touch the Petitioner Candle, saying:

Here Spirituality and Understanding move in to become a part of me. Let them become one with me so that I will never forget them.

With the Awl, inscribe the Red and White Candle with the words "Love" and "Honor." Dress it with Oil.
Light the Red and White Candle, and slowly move it inward to finally touch the Petitioner Candle, saying:

Here Love and Honor move in to become a part of me. Let them become one with me so that I will never forget them.

With the Awl, inscribe the Yellow Candle with the words "Wisdom" and "Confidence." Dress it with Oil.
Light the Yellow Candle, and slowly move it inward to finally touch the Petitioner Candle, saying:

Here Wisdom and Confidence move in to become a part of me. Let them become one with me so that I will never forget them.

Take up the Censer and swing it, censing the whole area around the altar, while rhythmically repeating the Key Word "Rebirth," and building up the energy to that focus. Replace the Censer and direct your energies toward the Petitioner Candle. Say:

I now start the adult phase of my life. I understand that with all advancements come responsibilities. First and foremost I will be responsible for myself, walking in love and truth, and seeking to do naught but good in this world. I accept my responsibilities with gladness and joy, and hope that I may fulfill all the expectations that others have of me. I ask God/Goddess/All-That-Is* to help me keep this vow.

Again cense the altar set-up while chanting the Key Word. Then sit and quietly meditate on your goals in life: where you want to go; what you want to achieve. Feel good about yourself and congratulate yourself.

Extinguish the candles in reverse order.

---

*This may be adapted for any particular religious persuasion, inserting the name(s) of the deity if desired.

XII

LAST WORDS
(or, "But I can't find any Juniper Berries!")

As I said in the beginning, High Magick generally takes a lot of work. It calls for time, patience, and—to a certain extent—expense. If you want to do the rituals properly (and I'm sure you do, otherwise you wouldn't be considering Advanced Candle Magick), then you will take the time and trouble to find all the ingredients that are needed. Some of those ingredients are not easy to come by—especially many of the herbs and oils designated—but that doesn't mean they are impossible to find.

Search for what you need. Go through your local phone book. Go to your public library and search the Yellow Pages of some of the big cities such as New York,

Chicago, Los Angeles, and New Orleans. Look under headings for Metaphysical, New Age, or Occult Stores, and also "Botanicas." Send for every metaphysical catalog you can lay hands on. (You'll find several advertised in *Fate* magazine, plus in the tabloids sold in supermarkets.) Call or write to anyone and everyone who might have an answer. If necessary, advertise for what you need in the classified sections of *Fate*, *New Worlds of Mind and Spirit*, and elsewhere.

If you really want what you desire, then you should be willing to put some effort into getting the ingredients for doing the appropriate ritual. Don't sit around crying, "but I can't find any juniper berries!" If you search long enough and hard enough you can find them, and everything else you need. Having said that, let me also say that it is possible to substitute for some items. In the rituals (Part Three), you will see that I frequently give alternatives. (See also, Table 12, "Substitutions," in the Appendix.)

You will find that preparation for a ritual takes far longer than the practice; but, as I pointed out earlier, most of that preparation is actually a part of the ritual. Take a pride in everything you make, from the candles to the wands, oils, and talismans. Put effort into it and that effort will become "power," and you will gain immeasurably.

Disposing of Candles, Poppets, and Other Symbols

What should you do with candles after the ritual? That is a question I get asked a lot. The short answer is that, once the ritual is finished, the candles, plackets, and even the poppets are no longer significant. They can simply be tossed away, and the candles burned as decorative pieces. I often hear gasps when I suggest this: "What about this poppet? It represents Bill. I can't toss away Bill!" No, of course you can't; but don't forget that it's only in the ritual situation that the poppet represents Bill. If you toss it out later, you are not doing anything *with intent* toward Bill. In the same way, if you burn an ex-ritual candle as a table ornament a week or so after having used it in a ritual, it is no longer being burned with any intent, and no longer represents someone or something.

However, there may be some items that *are* still representative after the actual ritual, if that was the original intention. Sometimes a poppet is made for an ongoing spell. For example, two love poppets tied together in ritual to keep love alive between the two people they represent, should be put away safely. A talisman for protection should be kept carefully.

In spite of what I say, there's no reason why you shouldn't play it safe if you feel strongly about it. If only as a psychological comfort, you can "de-fuse" everything you've used. Here is a simple ritual for doing just that.

Deconsecration Rite

With the Altar Candles (if you use them) on your altar, and some incense burning, lay the object—candle, poppet, placket—on the altar in front of you. Concentrate on the object, seeing it as it was consecrated in the ritual. If possible, see it surrounded by a ball of colored light; the color pertinent to the object (e.g., a poppet in the astral colors of the person represented, a money candle in a green light, or a love candle in a pink light). Then see that color slowly getting paler; slowly turning to white. If necessary direct the light from yourself into the object, driving out all significance and leaving it as pure, white light.

Take up the object and hold it in the smoke of the incense. Say:

> *Here do I hold a candle [poppet, whatever]. No longer does this represent anyone or anything. It is once again simply an object, signifying nothing. Anything that I or anyone else does to this object will have no relationship to the person or thing this used to represent. This candle is now pure and clean, cleansed of all energies.*

That is all you need to do. It negates what was done to the object during the ritual, and, because it is now out of the ritual situation, it is completely "clean."

The Power of Candle Magick

Candleburning Magick has been practiced almost as long as humankind has been in existence. It is effective and, perhaps more importantly, it is *safe*. You are not conjuring anyone or anything—no evil spirits, demons, or entities of any type. The Magickal power you use you draw from yourself (and/or from deity). You might say that it is the next step up from prayer. For many, prayer, whether aimed at specific deity or just at "whoever's out there," is little more than wishful thinking, or wishful asking. Sometimes the prayer is intense enough to generate energy and bring about results, and the prayer is "answered." The next step from plain prayer is the burning of a candle at the same time. This can be a great help in that you are now *doing* something, not just sitting and asking. You are putting energy into it.

Candleburning Magick is a step up from that. You are doing a lot of things; putting a lot of energy into it. Chances are, you are far more likely to get results. The final step would seem to be what we have covered here in this book.

Don't think the rituals given here are the only ones that you can use. I encourage you to write your own rituals; make your own candles; incorporate the colors and additives; use whatever supplementary items you feel will help. Take that final step along the High Magick path, and you will be doing everything possible to bring about what it is that you desire. You deserve to succeed—and I think you will!

APPENDIX

Table 1. Planetary Hours

SUNRISE

HOUR	Sun	Mon	Tue	Wed	Thu	Fri	Sat
1	[	@	N	O	m	T	R
2	T	R	[	@	N	O	m
3	O	m	T	R	[	@	N
4	@	N	O	m	T	R	[
5	R	[	@	N	O	m	T
6	m	T	R	[	@	N	O
7	N	O	m	T	R	[	@
8	[	@	N	O	m	T	R
9	T	R	[	@	N	O	m
10	O	m	T	R	[	@	N
11	@	N	O	m	T	R	[
12	R	[	@	N	O	m	T

SUNSET

Hour	Sun	Mon	Tue	Wed	Thu	Fri	Sat
1	m	T	R	[	@	N	O
2	N	O	m	T	R	[	@
3	[	@	N	O	m	T	R
4	T	R	[	@	N	O	m
5	O	m	T	R	[	@	N
6	@	N	O	m	T	R	[
7	R	[	@	N	O	m	T
8	m	T	R	[	@	N	O
9	N	O	m	T	R	[	@
10	[	@	N	O	m	T	R
11	T	R	[	@	N	O	m
12	O	m	T	R	[	@	N

[Sun, O Mercury, R Saturn, N Mars, T Venus, @ Moon, m Jupiter

Table 2. Properties of Planets

Sun

The Sun is first and foremost a masculine planet, full of vitality. It has determination, yet much kindness. It has a lot of heart and is capable of great love. It is an authority figure moving ever forward.

Key Words
Self-expression; Vitality

Associations
Creativity, fatherhood, children, games, royalty

Physical Associations
The heart and the spine

Positive Traits
Affectionate, creative, generous, love of children, love of life, quiet dignity

Negative Traits
Arrogant, over-bearing, condescending, domineering

Mercury (Uranus)

Mercury is quick-witted with an extremely active mind, good for research, explorations, analysis, judgment. Good for writers, teachers, orators.

Key Word
Communication

Associations
Travel, mental perception

Physical Associations
The brain, the intellect, nervous system, respiratory system

Positive Traits
Desire to learn and to teach, versatility, perception, intellectual, reasoning powers

Negative Traits
Inconsistent, argumentative, sarcastic, cynical, hypercritical

Saturn

Saturn is inhibited, persevering, cautious, often frustrated, taciturn, reserved.

Key Word
Limitation

Associations
Tenacity, slow change, inhibition, restriction, intolerance, law, mining, printing, dentistry, building and real estate, second-hand goods, agriculture, death

Physical Associations
Skin, bones, teeth, gall bladder, spleen

Positive Traits
Cautious, practical, thrifty, reliable, self-desciplined, patient

Negative Traits
Selfish, dogmatic, depressing, aloof

Mars (Pluto)

Mars is for action with great energy and courage. May be brutal and jealous—frequently the cause of sexual problems

Key Words
Energy; Initiative

Associations
Action, masculinity, aggression, weapons and tools, impulsiveness, loyalty, fear of the unknown, soldiers, surgeons, sportsmen, and craftsmen

Physical Associations
Adrenals, kidneys, urogenital, red blood corpuscles, muscles

Positive Traits
Defends the weak, is decisive, responsive, pioneering, freedom-loving

Negative Traits
Selfish, over-aggressive, brutal, unthinking, quarrelsome, rude

Venus (Neptune)

Very feminine; very much connected with love, friendship, and physical attraction.

Key Word
Harmony

Associations
Feminine influences, money, partnerships, possessions, the arts, beauty, clothing, fashion, feeling, peace-making, pleasures, musicians, jewelers, actors, dressmakers, artists, and nurses

Physical Associations
Throat, kidneys, lumbar region, parathyroids, feelings (especially of love)

Positive Traits
Kind and gentle, appreciative of beauty, tactful, adaptable, placid, lover

Negative Traits
Excessively romantic, effusive, impractical, indecisive, parasitical

Moon

A feminine figure. Very sensitive, emotional, domestic. A lover of water.

Key Words
Instinctive; Fluctuation; Responsive

Associations
Emotional disturbance, memory, home and family, ancestors, personal habits, nutrition, patriotism, public welfare

Physical Associations
Birth, motherhood, digestion, stomach, breasts, sympathetic nervous system, body fluids

Positive Traits
Patient, shrewd, tenacious, imaginative, maternal, good memory

Negative Traits
Moody, changeable, unreliable, gullible, narrow-minded, unforgiving

Jupiter

The planet of harmony, education, law, morals and religion, self-education.

Key Word
Expansion

Associations
Truth, knowledge, religion, education, languages, foreign countries, book publication, philosophy, languages, faith, good humor, learning through reading, bankers, judges, ecclesiastics

Physical Associations
Pituitary gland, liver

Positive Traits
Generous, optimistic, loyal, just, compassionate, good at
sports and languages

Negative Traits
Self-indulgent, extravagant, conceited, overly-optimistic,
extremist

Table 3. Days, Planetary Rulers, and Attributes

Monday	Moon	Ancestors, childbearing, dreams, healing, instinct, memory, merchandise, purity, theft, virginity
Tuesday	Mars	Enemies, initiation, loyalty, matrimony, prison, protection, war, wealth,
Wednesday	Mercury	Business, communication, debt, fear, loss, travel
Thursday	Jupiter	Clothing, desires, harvests, honor, marriage, oaths and treaties, riches
Friday	Venus	Beauty, family life, friendship, fruitfulness, growth, harmony, love, nature, pleasures, sexuality, strangers, waters
Saturday	Saturn	Building, doctrine, freedom, gifts, life, protection, real estate, sowing, tenacity
Sunday	Sun	Agriculture, beauty, creativity, fortune, guardianship, hope, money, self-expression, victory

Table 4. Symbolism of Colors

Red	Courage, health, sexual love, strength, vigor
Pink	Honor, love, morality
Orange	Adaptability, attraction, encouragement, stimulation
Yellow (gold)	Attraction, charm, confidence, persuasion, protection
White	Purity, sincerity, truth
Greenish-yellow	Anger, cowardice, discord, jealousy, sickness
Green	Fertility, finance, healing, luck
Brown	Hesitation, neutrality, uncertainty
Blue, light	Health, patience, tranquility, understanding
Blue, dark	Changeability, depression, impulsiveness
Violet	Healing, peace, spirituality
Purple	Ambition, business progress, power, tension
Silver (gray)	Cancellation, neutrality, stalemate
Black	Confusion, discord, evil, loss

Table 5. Astral Colors

Zodiac Sign	Birth Date	Primary Candle Color	Secondary Candle Color	Poppet Astral Colors
Aquarius	1/20–2/18	BLUE	Green	Indigo, electric blue
Pisces	2/19–3/20	WHITE	Green	Sea green, indigo
Aries	3/21–4/19	WHITE	Pink	Red (all shades)
Taurus	4/20–5/20	RED	Yellow	Yellow, pale blue, pink
Gemini	5/21–6/21	RED	Blue	Violet, yellow
Cancer	6/22–7/22	GREEN	Brown	Green, smoky gray
Leo	7/23–8/22	RED	Green	Orange
Virgo	8/23–9/22	GOLD	Black	Violet, dark gray, navy
Libra	9/23–10/22	BLACK	Blue	Yellow, pale blue, pink
Scorpio	10/23–11/21	BROWN	Black	Red, dark red, maroon
Sagittarius	11/22–12/21	GOLD	Red	Purple, dark blue
Capricorn	12/22–1/19	RED	Brown	Blue, dark gray

Table 6. Days of the Week

Monday	White
Tuesday	Red
Wednesday	Purple
Thursday	Blue
Friday	Green
Saturday	Black
Sunday	Yellow

Table 7. Magickal Properties
of Herbs

Anemone	Protects against sickness
Angelica	Lengthens life, protects from disease, exorcises evil
Basil	Protects from evil, aids love
Borage	Generates courage, lifts spirits
Caraway	Guards against theft, promotes love
Cedar chips	Attracts money
Cinquefoil	Brings love, aids in divination, protects from evil
Clover	Brings luck, wealth, prosperity
Comfrey	Aids healing
Cornflower	Promotes good eyesight
Dill	Protects from evil
Fennel	Purifies
Marjoram	Ensures happiness in the afterlife
Mugwort	Aleviates female disorders, shows the future, protects from wild beasts
Myrtle	For love and peace
Parsley	Protects from poison, promotes long life
Plantain	Cleanses and purifies

Rosemary	For loyalty, devotion, love, strength
Sage	Promotes health and long life
St. John's Wort	For exorcisms, dispells evil
Solomon's Seal	Heals wounds
Sunflower	To find a thief
Thyme	For courage, chivalry
Valerian	Restores peace, harmony, togetherness
Vervain	Reconciles enemies, protects from harm, ensures fidelity
Wild Thyme	Protects against nightmares

Recommended reading: ***Cunningham's Encyclopedia of Magical Herbs*** by Scott Cunningham (Llewellyn, 1985).

Table 8. Properties of Precious and Semi-Precious Stones

Agate (chalcedony variety): grounding; healing; distinguishes truth

Amazonite (feldspar): creativity; joy; psychic expander

Amber (burmite, pimetite, puccinite, ruminite): soothing; harmonizing; awakens kundalini

Amethyst (quartz): meditation; healing; dispels illusion; promotes psychic abilities, especially channeling; protective

Beryl: patience; humor; discipline

Bloodstone (heliotrope): reduces stress, emotional and mental; stimulates kundalini; psychic healer

Carnelian (chalcedony): grounds and aligns

Chrysolite (peridot, olivine): prevents nightmares; purifies; increases psychic awareness

Coral (calcium carbonate): stabilizer; positiveness

Diamond: panacea; covers full spectrum in psychic/spiritual matters

Emerald (beryl): dreams; meditation; tranquility; helps contact higher self

Garnet: general stimulant; compassion; grounding

Jade: wisdom; protection; courage; dispels negativity; protects

Lapis Lazuli (lazurite): promotes psychic abilities, contact with higher self

Lapis Linguis (azurite): meditation; promoting psychic abilities

Lapis Lingurius (malachite): protection from the "evil eye"

Moonstone (adularia variety of orthoclase): compassion; governs the affections; relieves stress

Opal: good for use with children; "the stone of love"; enhances intuition; amplifies chakra; protects

Pearl: meditation; soothing

Quartz Crystal: purity; spiritual protector; helps channeling; amplifier

Rose Quartz: creativity; self-confidence; eases tensions

Ruby (corundum): regeneration; spiritual devotion; integrity

Sardonyx (cryptocrystalline quartz): soothes emotional states

Topaz (alumino-fluoro-silicate): inspiration; soothing and calming; banishes nightmares; emotional balance; tranquility

Tourmaline (black): protection; imagination; intuition; overcomes fear; clairvoyance

Tourmaline (pink/green): regeneration; balance and harmony; compassion; empathy; rejuvenation

Turquoise (copper-and-aluminum phosphate): communication; peace of mind; calming; loyalty

Zircon (hyacinth): self-esteem; strength; storage of psychic power

Table 9. Magickal Squares

```
S  I  T  U  R        O  R  I  O  N
I  R  A  P  E        R  A  V  R  O
T  A  R  A  G        I  V  A  V  I
U  P  A  L  A        O  R  V  A  R
R  E  G  A  N        N  O  I  R  O
```

Health   **Wealth**

```
S  A  L  O  M        D  E  B  A  M
A  R  E  P  O        E  R  E  R  A
L  E  M  E  L        B  E  R  E  B
O  P  E  R  A        A  R  E  R  E
M  O  L  A  S        M  A  B  E  D
```

For the love   **For the love**
of a female   **of a male**

```
A  M  P  A
R  O  L  A
M  P  A  R
O  L  A  M
```

For Protection

Table 10. Native American Color Symbolism

There is variation between the different Native American peoples on the symbolism of colors. Here is the symbolism of the Pathway of Peace, from the philosophy of the ancient Seneca people (as taught by Seneca Elder Twyler Nitsch). It is an example of how color symbolism is used among the Native Americans to help direct their lives. The first seven colors were viewed as stepping stones one walked along to gain wisdom.

Red	Faith	Communication
Yellow	Love	Overcoming challenges through unconditional love
Blue	Intuition	Using intuition to teach and serve
Green	Will	Living willfully
Pink	Creativity	Working
White	Magnetism	Sharing
Purple	Wisdom	Gratitude/healing
Orange	Learning	Kinship
Gray	Honoring	Friendship
Brown	Knowing	Self-discipline
Rose	Seeing	Motivation
Black	Hearing	Harmony; listening
Crystal	Clarity	Wholeness

Table 11. Asian Color Symbolism

According to the teachings of Feng-Shuí, the following are the symbolic meanings of various colors:

Red	Happiness, marriage, prosperity
Pink	Marriage
Yellow	Against evil, for the dead, geomantic blessings
Green	Eternity, family, harmony, health, peace, posterity
Blue	Self-cultivation, wealth
Purple	Wealth
White	Children, helpful people, marriage, mourning, peace, purity, travel
Gold	Strength, wealth
Gray	Helpful people, travel
Black	Career, evil influences, knowledge, mourning, penance, self-cultivation

Table 12. Substitutions

Scott Cunningham (*The Magic of Incense, Oils and Brews*, Llewellyn, 1986) groups herbs according to their properties, to facilitate finding substitutes (for example, apple could be substituted for rosemary in a love spell, but not in a healing spell; similarly, musk could be substituted for tonka in a ritual to attain courage, but it couldn't in a rite for wealth).

Courage
Musk, sweetpea, thyme, tonka

Divination or development of psychic powers
Acacia, bay, camphor, cinnamon, citron, clove, galangal, honeysuckle, lemon grass, mace, mastic, nutmeg, orange, orris, peppermint, rose, star anise, thyme, wormwood

Exorcism
Angelica, basil, clove, cumin, dragon's blood, frankincense, fumitory, garlic, heliotrope, horehound, juniper, lilac, mallow, mint, mistletoe, myrrh, pepper, pine, rosemary, rue, sagebrush, sandalwood, snapdragon, thistle, yarrow

Healing
Allspice, angelica, bay, calamus, carnation, cedar, cinnamon, citron, eucalyptus, fennel, gardenia, heliotrope, lemon balm, lime, mint, mugwort, myrrh, pepper, peppermint, pine, rose, rosemary, sandalwood, spearmint, thyme, violet, willow, yerba santa

Love

Apple, apricot, basil, cardamom, catnip, chamomile, chick-weed, cinnamon, clove, copal, coriander, dill, dragon's blood, gardenia, geranium, ginger, hibiscus, jasmine, juniper, lavender, lemon, lemon balm, lemon verbena, lime, lotus, marjoram, mastic, mimosa, myrtle, orange, orchid, pansy, peppermint, plumeria, rose, rosemary, sarsaparilla, spearmint, thyme, tonka, vanilla, vervain, vetivert, yarrow

Purification

Anise, avens, bay, benzoin, cedar, coconut, copal, fennel, gum Arabic, hyssop, lavender, lemon, lemon verbena, mimosa, parsley, peppermint, rosemary, sagebrush, thyme, tobacco, vervain

Wealth

Allspice, almond, basil, bergamot, calamus, cedar, chamomile, cinnamon, cinquefoil, clove, clover, dill, elder, galangal, ginger, heliotrope, honeysuckle, jasmine, mint, myrtle, nutmeg, oak, orange, pine, sassafras, tonka, vervain, vetivert, woodruff

Table 13. Magickal Alphabets

Theban

A	B	C	D	E	F	G	H	I,J	K	L	M	N	O	P

Symbol designating end of a sentence

Passing the River

A	B	C	D	E	F	G	H	I,J	K	L	M	N	O,Q	P

Angelic

A	B	C	D	E	F	G	H	I,J	K	L	M	N	O,Q	P

Malachim

A	B	C	D	E	F	G	H	I,J	K	L	M	N	O,Q	P

Seax-Wica Runes

A	B	C	D	E	F	G	H	I,J	K	L	M	N	O,Q	P

Egyptian Heiroglyphics

A	B	C CH K TSH	D	E	F PH	G	H	I	J	KH	L	M	N

Pictish

A	B	C	CH	D	E	G	GH	H	I	J	K	L	M	N

Q	R	S	T	U,V	X	Y	Z

R	S	T	U,V	W	X	Y	Z

R	S	T	U,V	W	X	Y	Z

R	S	T	U,V	W	X	Y	Z

R	S	T	U	V	W	X	Y	Z	NG	GH	EA	AE	OE	TH

O	P	Q	R	S	S	SH	T	TCH	TH	U	V W	Y

NG	O	P	Q	R	S	SH	T	TH	U	V	W	X	Y	Z

GET MORE AT LLEWELLYN.COM

Visit us online to browse hundreds of our books and decks, plus sign up to receive our e-newsletters and exclusive online offers.

- Free tarot readings • Spell-a-Day • Moon phases
- Recipes, spells, and tips • Blogs • Encyclopedia
- Author interviews, articles, and upcoming events

GET SOCIAL WITH LLEWELLYN

Find us on   @LlewellynBooks

www.Facebook.com/LlewellynBooks

GET BOOKS AT LLEWELLYN

LLEWELLYN ORDERING INFORMATION

Order online: Visit our website at www.llewellyn.com to select your books and place an order on our secure server.

Order by phone:
- Call toll free within the US at 1-877-NEW-WRLD (1-877-639-9753)
- We accept VISA, MasterCard, American Express, and Discover.

Order by mail:
Send the full price of your order (MN residents add 6.875% sales tax) in US funds plus postage and handling to: Llewellyn Worldwide, 2143 Wooddale Drive, Woodbury, MN 55125-2989

POSTAGE AND HANDLING

STANDARD (US):(Please allow 12 business days)
$30.00 and under, add $6.00.
$30.01 and over, FREE SHIPPING.

CANADA:
We cannot ship to Canada. Please shop your local bookstore or Amazon Canada.

INTERNATIONAL:
Customers pay the actual shipping cost to the final destination, which includes tracking information.

Visit us online for more shipping options. Prices subject to change.

FREE CATALOG!

To order, call
1-877-
NEW-WRLD
ext. 8236
or visit our
website